I0123292

Charlie

Don Allison

Published by Don Allison, 2022.

While every precaution has been taken in the preparation of this book, the publisher assumes no responsibility for errors or omissions, or for damages resulting from the use of the information contained herein.

CHARLIE

First edition. November 25, 2022.

Copyright © 2022 Don Allison.

ISBN: 978-0974000244

Written by Don Allison.

Also by Don Allison

Charlie

Table of Contents

Chapter 1
Bellflower

Charlie had no idea his life might take the direction it did. Born in 1887, his mother died soon after, leaving his father, Derwen Owens[1], to raise Charlie and two daughters alone. His father struggled for a meager living on his hardscrabble farm in northeast Missouri. Charlie's survival as a toddler can be attributed to the care he received from his sisters, young though they were.

By 1891, unable to support them any longer, Derwen surrendered his children to an orphanage near St. Louis where they would await adoption. Charlie was 4, growing up with a fading recollection of his real father.

Life was hard for other children too. With disease and poverty and so many families moving west, many children found themselves abandoned to adoption, with orphanages able to provide little more than the bare minimum of care. Many were little more than labor pools for sweatshops. Orphanages enforced strict rules, and the social hierarchy among the children placed there added to their difficulty. The "rule of the jungle" prevailed. To survive, one had to be strong. Charlie was strong.

Girls were more desirable for adoption than boys; still it was four years before Charlie's sisters were adopted. He was eight then, and never saw nor heard from them again.

Another four years passed before Charlie finally found his new family, although it wasn't the wonderful experience one might hope for. Charlie was twelve when adopted by John Allison and his second wife, Elmira. Allison's first marriage had produced a daughter, Annie, who was, by then, married, leaving the couple to tend their farm alone. Thus, their search for a son.

The Allisons made no secret of wanting Charlie solely for the labor he could provide. Elmira was a stern taskmaster who drove him hard, resorting to lashing him with whatever was handy, whether it be a switch, a board or a broom handle. John was little better, beating him with his fist whenever he felt the need or desire. Such treatment shaped and strengthened Charlie for the future.

The soil was poor at the Allison farm, eventually playing out, and forcing them to give up and move on. Packing what they could into a large Conestoga-style wagon, and with Charlie on foot herding their few cows and pigs, they headed south where they hoped the land was better.

It took them nearly two weeks to reach Bellflower, Missouri, a small village 80 miles west of St. Louis. Continuing westward through prairie grasslands, they arrived at the farm of JW Bean and his wife, Mary.

JW had seen them in the distance as they arrived in the valley, and hailed the Allison's, inviting them to water and rest their animals. It was here that Charlie, then fourteen, met the girl who would eventually become his wife.

Lola at 12

Lola was then twelve. She was the youngest of JW's nine children, with only Lola and three brothers yet on the farm. She watched from the fence overlooking the garden while her father and John Allison spoke of the land and prospects in that area. Mary and Elmira visited while Lola's brothers helped Charlie tend the animals and got acquainted.

The two men discussed farming at length before Allison decided to settle on a deserted farmstead that JW had suggested for him. It lay another two miles west, and Bean, glad to have neighbors, agreed to help repair the rundown and abandoned farm and to help prepare it for the coming fall and winter. He said he would send one or another of his boys as need arose and as he could.

While these discussions took place, Lola kept her eyes on Charlie, seeing in him a young man who appeared short in stature, especially standing beside her long and lanky brothers. He was powerfully built though, with a deep chest and broad shoulders. His hands, especially for a man so young, were large from hard work. Charlie carried himself in a confident manner belying his age. Lola was taken by him immediately, never dreaming of what lay ahead.

Chapter 2
Bellflower to Wellsville

Spring of 1902 found the Allisons breaking ground for planting. Having settled on the abandoned farmstead suggested by JW, and with his help, they were able to make the old buildings serviceable. And now, again with help, they were fully settled into their new home and planting their crops.

Charlie had had little schooling since leaving the orphanage. Most of his time was spent working as the Allisons demanded, although, this first winter here, he did take advantage of several opportunities to attend school. Charlie dreamt of making more of his life than farming could provide and knew he needed more education, though he would get little more formal education.

He rode his pony four miles to the one-room country schoolhouse, tying it outside as many of the other children did. And, because his route took him past the Bean farm, Lola often rode behind him on his pony. She may have been another reason he attended school.

Many of the schoolchildren believed the rumor that Charlie was a Roma, or "Gypsy," due in part to the style of wagon they arrived in and, in part from Elmira's dark complexion, derived from her Native American blood. Socially, Romas were considered as low as Blacks and Native Americans. This prejudice led to numerous arguments and fights for Charlie whenever he was in town, and even with his teacher, Karl Lang, a tall, thin man who often tried to embarrass him in front of class.

As winter turned to spring, Charlie decided he'd had enough of his teacher and of learning, and he told his teacher so. The resulting dispute found Charlie faced with an angry man threatening to whip Charlie for his impudence. But Charlie, then sixteen and strong as an ox, yanked Lang's switch away and lashed him with it, literally driving the teacher from the school. Charlie then calmly reentered the building and told the other children they could go home now. School was over. And so was Charlie's formal education.

While Charlie was relatively unschooled, he wasn't stupid. In fact, he was a quick study. He learned everything necessary for a man of that era and more. He was very mechanically inclined and could build or repair whatever was needed. He had quickly taken to blacksmithing with a forge JW had set up on his farm, which further added to Charlie's physical strength. JW was impressed by the speed with which Charlie picked up all manner of skills. But Charlie's desire to learn was driven by an ambition to get away from the Allisons and to be on his own. But it wasn't yet time. He still had to earn some money, something not easily done on a farm.

Fortunately for Charlie, when he helped the Bean family, as neighbors often did, JW sometimes paid him for doing a little extra. It wasn't much, but over time this bit of cash made a big difference. JW knew Charlie wanted to get away, and how he had been treated by his foster-parents. He may possibly have known, and approved of, the blooming relationship between Charlie and Lola.

Still, several years passed before Charlie saved enough to implement his plans. He wanted to get away from the farm and move to a big city where there was more opportunity. What he would do once there, he hadn't fully thought out, and it wasn't that important to him. The numerous skills he had developed would help him in many vocations.

A day came when Charlie and Lola's brother Ralph were sent to Bellflower for supplies. Eager to be on their way, Charlie eagerly climbed onto the buckboard where Ralph was at the reins. The ride would take well over an hour and the day promised to be warm. The horse acted eager too, as though glad to be away from the farm and on the move. With a "Heyup!" the young men were away in a flurry of dust.

The horse soon settled into a gentle pace and the boys shared stories. "I was born here," said Ralph. "Never been more'n twenty mile myself. You though, you come from up north. Seen a lot of country?" he asked.

"Seen enough," Charlie replied. "Enough to know I don't aim on staying around here any longer than I have to. Don't like farmin'. Figure to be on my own as soon as I can. Be a while though, I s'pect."

"Yeah?" Ralph said, "Well, I'll be stayin' on the farm, I guess. Being the youngest, it'll be mine someday. My brothers all plan on leavin' before too long themselves, and the girls'll get themselves married like the others did. Besides. The old man'll need my help as he gets older."

"Uh-huh," grunted Charlie. "Well, life is tough. To keep alive, you gotta be tougher. And I plan to be alive, somewhere else."

"Don't much care about your folks, do you?"

"They ain't my folks. Remember them telling I was adopted? The old man needed another hand on the farm. That's all I am to him, another hand. And his woman? She's about as mean as they come. No. I ain't staying no longer than I have to."

"Whyn't you go now then?"

"Ain't got a dime, that's why. Don't get nuthin' for the work I do. Someday though. Someday..."

The two rode along in silence for a while as the sun climbed higher overhead. Finally, the village came into sight. Ralph was familiar with Bellflower, but this was Charlie's first trip to the village. In fact, he had been in few towns in his fourteen years. So, this was an adventure he looked forward to. Settled in 1887, the same year Charlie was born, fewer than 300 people called Bellflower home. Yet, it was a disappointment to Charlie when they arrived. He saw only a scattering of homes, a blacksmith shop, a post office inside the general store, and a saloon.

"Over there's the general store," said Ralph. "Ought to find what we need there."

Entering the dimly lit store, Charlie saw two men sitting at a small table, playing checkers. He nodded to them. One, wearing a straw hat, nodded in return, the other, a stout man wearing dirty bib overalls just glanced at Charlie for a moment, then returned to their game.

Shelves of dry and canned goods lined one side of the building. The other wall held drawers filled with fasteners, ammunition, and other small items. Tools, hardware, and farm related supplies stood in the middle and the very front of the store appeared to be reserved for bolts of cloth and various sundry items including a small supply of manufactured clothing.

The boys each told the proprietor what items they needed, then while waiting for them to be gathered, they watched the men at their checker game.

The man big man wearing bibs moved a checker up one square and immediately his opponent jumped it with a loud, "Hah! Gotcha!" Charlie made the mistake of laughing and saying, "I saw that one coming."

"You did, did you, boy?" said the bibbed man with a scowl. "I s'pose you could do better."

"Maybe so. I saw it. You didn't."

At that remark, the man began to rise when the "the proprietor interrupted. "Boys. I got your things ready. Come, haul 'em out."

Charlie hoisted the hundred-pound sack of flour onto one shoulder and started for the door. On his way out, the man in bibs stuck his foot out causing Charlie to trip and tumble through the door. "Shoulda saw that!" he said with a laugh.

Angered, Charlie rose from the ground and headed straight for the big man who had risen from his seat to meet the challenge. "S'matter kid. Trip over your big feet?"

The man stood a full head taller than Charlie's five feet-six, yet Charlie charged at him, ducking a meaty fist that was aimed for his face. Charlie's shoulder slammed into the big man's chest, driving him back and onto the table. With a crash, the table collapsed as checkers flew across the floor.

"Enough!" yelled the store's owner as Charlie quickly stood, prepared to continue the contest. "Enough!" the owner repeated. "Both of you." Charlie stood over the man, his fists doubled, while the big man rolled onto his hands and knees, preparing to stand. He waved at Charlie and said, "That's enough, kid. We've done enough. You jumped my king. You win."

Having gained the respect of at least one man, Ralph and Charlie completed loading their goods into the wagon and began their return journey.

"Kind of a short fuse, huh?" said Ralph.

"Well, the son-of-a-bitch deserved it," Charlie replied.

"Well, yeah. Can't argue with you there. Don't think I'd want to argue with you either," Ralph said with a grin.

"Like I told you, life is hard. To get by, you gotta be tougher. I figure, if I let that guy get by with it once, he'd sure as hell do it again. Besides, I'm done gettin' pushed around."

This was the first scrape Charlie had been in since his fight with the schoolteacher, yet word circulated that he was a troublemaker. As a result, on his next trip to Bellflower, he was, once more faced with a challenger. While men shunned him, two boys – young men – sought him out to gain notoriety for themselves by "whipping" Charlie Allison in a fight. It didn't happen. Charlie just wouldn't be "whipped." But these encounters cemented in him the knowledge that he had to be tough to make it in this world.

Soon the time came when Charlie finally had enough - enough of the challenges, enough of the farm, and enough money to try to make it on his own. So, that spring of 1908, he said to Lola, "Let's go," and they did. In her words, "Charlie and me decided to run off together that spring, and we done it."

They "done it." Taking the few possessions each had and Charlie's pony, they headed for Wellsville, Missouri, where Charlie immediately found work as a carpenter, and where they were married in August of that year. But their challenges were just beginning.

Chapter 3
Wellsville and Beyond

Having broken the tethers that bound him to his foster parents, Charlie was finally on his own. It wasn't the hard work on the farm that he opposed; it was the constant threats and insults he had been forced to endure. But no more. Or so he hoped.

Charlie found work in Wellsville, 17 miles away, not just as a carpenter, but at a variety of tasks, though each job seemed to last only a short while. He also found that those he worked for were just as demanding of him as his foster father. Charlie, not one to take orders easily, desired to be given a task and left to do it without constant oversight.

In Wellsville, he and Lola found lodging in a boardinghouse. It wasn't much; it provided a room, but little else. The food was spartan, oatmeal for breakfast and stew for supper, day after day.

At first, the other boarders were unfriendly, coarse, and crude. When food was brought to the table, greedy hands quickly ladled it onto their plates until it was soon gone.

"Grab me some, Charlie, before it's all gone," Lola complained. "These folks take all there is before I can even reach for it."

"Catch-as-catch-can, lady," retorted one of the boarders, a man. "Ain't nobody gonna hand it to ya."

But Charlie, in a rage, said, "No more! After this, when food is brought out, you," he said, pointing to another man's wife, "will dish it out so that everyone gets a fair share."

Startled by this, the woman simply looked at Charlie while the first man began to stand in protest, saying, "Who the hell are you to say what to do?"

Charlie, raising his meaty fist, shook it at him and said, "This says so!"

11

Grumbling, but unwilling to do more than that, the man relented and sat back down.

Yet, as time passed, mealtime became a more civil affair, and others agreed it was a welcome change.

But Lola never forgot the man's comment, and she repeated it often to her children so that it became deeply rooted in them. "Ain't nobody gonna hand nothin' to ya in this world," she would say. "You gotta stand on your own two feet and fight if you're gonna have anything!"

Some months after the incident at the supper table, while alone in the privacy of their room, Lola complained again to Charlie about the food, saying, "All it is, is mush. I can fix a lot better'n that."

"Well, we'll see," Charlie said. "You might get a chance to prove it the next place we go."

Charlie Allison

He was already thinking of moving on, and when the time was right, they would. His jobs in Wellsville provided them a scant living with little more than food on the table.

That winter, Lola announced she was pregnant. That settled things for Charlie; the time to move was near. After daughter Velma Geraldine was born, they traveled 150 miles, to Nilwood, Illinois.

Charlie was promised a steady job using his carpentry skills with Linro Products in Nilwood. But the job turned out to be dirty, monotonous work in an unheated factory where workers baked in summer and nearly froze in the winter. He also discovered that the foreman and some of his cronies were a rough and demanding lot who used bullying tactics and threats to force men to work extra hours without extra pay. "D'you want this job or not?" the boss demanded.

Want it? No. But Charlie needed it, at least for a time.

Working long hours for less pay than promised, Charlie was forced to find added income. Lola agreed to take in borders, and to prove she could "fix a lot better'n that," as she had said in Wellsville.

Having rented a small house, they soon had a few laborers sharing it with them. This arrangement helped them financially, and Lola was able to "fix up some food" better than what they had when they were boarders themselves. Still, the arrangement was far from satisfactory.

Charlie found that being on his own had not given him the freedom he wished for when he left home. Wherever he went, it seemed, there were those who would bully and threaten, who used their authority to dictate. So, after a little more than a year at Linro, he decided he'd had enough. He began looking for the right time to move on again.

Illinois isn't known for its coal industry today[2], but coal mining was a major industry in west-central Illinois at the time. Several communities had grown up around the mines, and Charlie, disillusioned with what he'd experienced so far, decided to try mining. Working in a coal mine hardly sounds like a step up, but to Charlie anything was better than working for Linro.

There were twenty-two coal mines in Macoupin County. Charlie decided to move his family another 6 miles to Girard to try his hand in one there.

And it was there that he met a man called, variously, Bryan or Byron Bolton[3]. He would be known by many other names through the coming years and would assure Charlie a behind-the-scenes view of historic events to come.

Chapter 4
Girard

When Charlie began working at the Girard coal mine, he found the work was both hard and dirty, but the pay was better than at Linro. Also, his foreman wasn't on him all the time, although that may have been because he was just one of many other miners.

Here again, as in Nilwood, he rented a large house while Lola took in boarders. Bolton was one of them. The same age as Charlie, Bolton grew up on a farm near Girard where he made and supplied corn liquor for the miners. As coal mining grew, so did the demand for liquor. The operation of stills had long been a way for farmers to convert their corn to cash. This provided Bolton the opportunity to organize area farmers so that he became a distributor of the liquor produced by them. While it was against the law it was considered a legitimate business by most people, though not by the government, which lost tax revenue from it. Bolton, however, wasn't concerned about the law.

He convinced Charlie that the boarding house would be an ideal place to sell bootleg liquor. Bolton, a fancy dresser, had other interests too. He was a union organizer, a gambler, and loved to chase women. He was a big man among big men, standing over six feet tall. Powerful and willing to use his strength, he was not one to trifle with. And since he and Charlie were so much alike, they quickly became fast friends.

Bolton knew many of the miners and their bosses, and it was through his influence that enabled Charlie to get a better job at the mine, removing from the stooped-over task of working coal. Charlie's duties became that of making and mending harnesses for the mules used in the mine[4]. This was before electric cars were in operation, when coal was removed by mule cart.

Some mules, afraid of the utter darkness within the mines, had to be led by a man walking ahead of them carrying a lantern. Some mules, when reaching the surface, trembled at the glow of sunshine, and leapt about as though mad with joy. When this occurred, the mules became very hard to handle, and it was difficult to get them back into the dark mines. For this reason, many were kept stabled within the mines their entire lives.

To help tend the mules, Charlie hired boys, 10 and 11 years old, to transport food to, and waste from, the underground room that served as the stables. Each mule driver had to be in the mines by 4 AM to curry, feed, and tend to his mules, with the miners coming later.

Single mules were used to pull cars from the working face. Once reaching the gangways, these cars were hitched together and a two- or three-mule team hauled them to the main gangways where a six-mule team pulled 25 or more cars to the tipple, or head, where they were dumped. It was hard work for both the men and the mules, even though the floors in the mines sloped downward toward the shaft entrance.

Work in the mines was long and tedious. The dangers were many. Explosions were commonplace and strong enough to knock a man down, or worse. These explosions were often caused when pockets of methane gas were touched off by the miners' carbide lamps. The threat of cave-ins also haunted the pits, and every miner kept an ear cocked for the creaking sounds of a roof about to give way. Pockets of carbon monoxide or "black damp" could suffocate a man in minutes, and heavily laden coal cars rolling through dimly lit tunnels were often fatal traps for the careless.

Each man worked stooped-over, covered in sweat and dust in the hot, stale air with no other light but that of his lamp. On top of that, their work was far from steady.

Depending on orders for coal, miners might work only two or three days a week. Demand varied with the seasons and with the needs of railroads and factories. This meant that, at thirty-five cents an hour, men were often lucky to earn ten dollars in a week[5]. But, for Charlie, though his job was hot and monotonous, his pay for mending harnesses was somewhat better than that of the average miner. And while he did a little better, with such meager pay and irregular hours, Charlie considered moving on again.

Coincidently, Bolton had also been thinking ahead. At the dinner table one night he said, "Charlie, I got some things going for me. I don't plan on being here forever, and I like you. You've got a good head on your shoulders. You've helped me sell my stuff here, and I'll need a fellow like you when I move on. How about it?"

"Bryan, I don't figure on working these mines the rest of my life either. Ain't no future in it. Just an early death. Whatcha got in mind?"

With the discussion that followed, Charlie's future was set in motion. In the spring they would take that next step.

Chapter 5

Death and Troubles

Later, in the winter of 1912-13, Charlie received news that his foster father had died. John Allison had been in Nilwood when he died suddenly.

"He was crossing the street," folks said, "when he just keeled over."

Charlie was neither shocked nor saddened by this news and chose to do nothing about it. But Lola convinced him that the right thing was to attend the funeral. "After all," she said, "it's just four miles to Nilwood. We can take the interurban[6]."

The interurban trolley, or Illinois Traction System, offered electric passenger service from St. Louis to Peoria. It provided cheap and comfortable transport for people having no other convenient way of getting from town to town. Charlie knew the man running the car they rode in

as "Jitney Jim."

Arriving in Nilwood, they found the roads so muddy and rutted they had to walk to the cemetery while a team of four horses pulled the hearse through the mud-clogged road. But even the horses got bogged down in the mire. Some of the men, Charlie included, had to help push the hearse at times. Lola complained at this, saying, "Charlie! Just look at you. You're gonna ruin your good clothes." To which he replied, "I don't care if they do get wrecked. I just want to see the old man planted good and deep." Such was his bitterness toward his foster father.

Charlie's feeling toward Elmira, his foster mother, was no better. With John Allison dead and Elmira's health failing, she was unable to take care of the farm herself and needed a place to live. Lola mentioned this to Charlie.

"I don't care if she stays on that farm and rots," Charlie said. "She's not moving in with us. She made my life a living hell then, and I'm not about to help her now."

But Lola knew how difficult life might be for a woman alone and took pity on her, arguing that, despite how badly the Allisons treated Charlie, if nothing else they had supplied him food, shelter, and clothing, so Elmira should be entitled to at least that much.

"Charlie! You can't be so heartless that you'd let a poor woman die like that. Not even if they did treat you bad. It's just not human to turn your back on somebody like that." Seeing no alternative, Charlie relented, and Elmira was invited to live with them, adding to their burdens.

Not long after, their troubles grew still worse. The mine closed. Men left town overnight to look for work. Charlie and Lola, still having to pay rent on the boarding house, were suddenly without income from his job at the mine or from boarders. Plans made with Bolton appeared to have evaporated, forcing them to move once again.

Virden lay six miles north of Girard. With three coal mines still in operation, it had an influx of out-of-work miners seeking jobs. Charlie was forced to take the only job he could find, building chicken crates at fifty cents a day. Being without money, he and Lola were forced to live in the only thing available to them, a tent. This was not unusual for miners at that time.

Each summer, the demand for coal for home heating dropped to a fraction of its wintertime levels[7]. So severe were these warm-weather slowdowns that many mines closed each summer and reopened toward fall. Such was true here.

Many of the county's 3,500 miners found their potential incomes slashed by forced idleness so that they earned less than $600 (4) a year. One miner was heard to say, "We never made any money when we was striking, and we never made any when we wasn't." Miners often bought their groceries on credit and let rent and other bills pile up while hoping the mines reopened before their creditors' patience ran out.

Charlie's worries were piling up too, while at the same time his patience was wearing thin. Once again, Bolton appeared. Still following the miners and selling bootleg liquor, he came to Charlie and Lola's aid with money enough for them to rent a place where they could take in boarders and sell his liquor again. This revived Charlie's and Bolton's earlier plans as summer passed and the mines reopened.

Chapter 6
Virden - Powder Monkey

Soon, Charlie's boarding house began to fill. That's when that Shorty Knudson appeared. Shorty was another friend of Bolton's, and a Teamster who had helped him organize the miners into a union. Because of that, he had pull within the mining community.

Virden had had a long history of mining troubles and strikes. It was the site of a major uprising[8] years earlier. The Chicago-Virden Coal Company hired armed guards to accompany a group of African American strikebreakers brought in from Birmingham, Alabama. Their purpose was to restart production, but armed strikers began shooting when the train arrived. During the melee, five guards and seven miners were killed, and more than thirty strikers were wounded. No one knows how many strikebreakers were injured.

After such a violent confrontation, the mine owners capitulated and accepted the unionization of the area's coal mines so that, in the end, the miners won out and became a very close-knit community.

Not everyone was close-knit, however. Sometimes squabbles between men turned violent. Such was a fight between two miners at Charlie's boarding house when one pulled a pistol on the other. Seeing what was about to happen, Charlie stepped in to try to stop the fight, grabbing the man who held the pistol. In the resulting melee, the gun went off, striking Charlie in the leg.

That ended the fight. Charlie, though wounded, took the gun away from the man and threw him out. Later, the man returned to apologize, and nothing more was done.

Charlie's wound was in his upper thigh, causing considerable loss of blood. Luckily, the bullet missed bone and major blood vessels, although damaging the muscles of his leg upon its exit. Over time, the wound healed, but it took several years for Charlie to recover fully.

Not long after, Bolton convinced Shorty to arrange for Charlie to be hired as a "powder monkey[9]," delivering explosives to the mine. This was something a man could do while healing from an injury. It also meant Charlie's day was just starting when others were leaving the mine at the end of their day, for it was then that blasting took place. The shot-firers had to drill several holes into the coal face [10]and pack them with black powder charges. Once ready, they lit the fuses and blasted the coal from the face, allowing dust and gasses to dissipate overnight.

One might think that coal miners simply loosen pure coal and haul it out, but there are other things mixed in with that coal, such as slate and sulfur and rock. These had to be separated from the coal and discarded into what was called the "gob[11]," a pile of waste that was left behind. Then the coal was hauled past walls dripping with black water and a blackness so deep it left one feeling as though he were floating in a vast void.

It wasn't long after Charlie returned to work in the mine that Shorty fell down an air shaft and was badly injured. He had various bruises and lacerations that healed quickly enough, but his broken leg and back injuries proved severe enough to prevent him from ever returning to mining.

Charlie would not allow his friend to go without help, especially since Shorty had done so much to help him. Besides, Shorty was a bachelor with no family and no one else to rely on, so Charlie told Lola, "We're taking him in."

But this time Lola argued, "Charlie, we don't have no more room. Where we going to put him?"

"Make room! He's a friend, and he's staying here." And that was that.

So, it fell to Lola, although she was pregnant again, to care for Shorty as well as young "Goldie" (as daughter Velma was called for her yellow hair) and Elmira, whose health continued to fail.

As Shorty recovered enough to be increasingly mobile, he and Charlie tended Bolton's bootlegging business in the mining community while Bolton traveled north to Chicago where his personal contacts were expanding.

"Networking" is a term often used today, but its origins go back a long way, and Bolton was a master of the craft. His connections with others were boosted by his gift of gab, as well as by his vision for the future. That vision would decide Charlie's future as well.

Chapter 7

The War Years

Lola gave birth to a baby boy in January of 1914 with the aid of her neighbors. Naming him Orin, Lola and Charlie would soon be calling him Buddy, and eventually, as he grew, just Bud. Buddy added to Lola's already busy schedule of caring for Shorty, Goldie, and the ailing Elmira, all while providing meals for the boarders.

Charlie's work in the mine continued, although the amount of gob[12] was beginning to exceed the coal harvested, and if another coal vein wasn't soon discovered, this mine would shut down. There was already talk among the miners about where they might move to next, while some, anticipating the mine's closure, had already left.

Charlie and Shorty continued to provide alcohol to those who remained, while Bolton spent more time in Chicago planning his next move. The income from liquor was drying up because there were fewer miners, and those left had less money to spend. Work at the mine continued to decline until, by spring, there were too few miners to justify fueling their thirst for alcohol. It just didn't pay. It was time to do something else.

By midsummer, the mine closed. Charlie could have moved on to another, but he was tired of mining. He heard of the need for men in the wheat fields of North Dakota, Kansas, and Minnesota. These were the chief wheat states at the time, with the harvest of spring planted wheat lasting from July through September[13]. Charlie made his decision. He left Lola to care for the others while he joined the wheat harvest in North Dakota.

His was a propitious move, for millions of European farmers were in the army due to World War I. This left those countries unable to produce enough food. Accordingly, the price of wheat shot up. This meant that Americans harvesting wheat and other crops worked long hours for days on end. With Charlie receiving good wages working the harvest, he was able to send some of his pay

back to support Lola and their children.

Bolton, meanwhile, had made the most of his connections, making him a soldier in what was to become a historic period in Chicago over the next decade, a period in which Charlie would play a role.

Meanwhile, Elmira's health deteriorated drastically, so she moved to live with her daughter, Annie Tannahill, in Franklin, Illinois. Annie and her husband had adult children, so they had the room and ability to supply better care for Elmira. This was a blessing for Lola, who still had the responsibility of running the boarding house, since Shorty had recovered from his injuries enough that he found a job he could do, and he moved on.

Charlie continued to follow the wheat harvest until completion, then he returned to Illinois. But without a mining job waiting for him, he had to find another kind of work. And he did. He was hired to deliver coal to households through the winter. It didn't pay much, but was better than nothing, especially as there were no longer any miners to provide rooms or alcohol for.

The year 1917 looked as though it would be even harder. Charlie was without a regular job but, being adept at many trades, was usually able to find some way to earn money as he waited for the next wheat harvest to begin in July. But then, as Charlie prepared to leave for North Dakota and another harvest season, he received word that Elmira died. Uncaring of her death, and with no further thought of her, he headed west, leaving Lola to care for their children.

Combines were not yet invented, and reaper-binders were used in the wheat fields. Invented a few years earlier by C B Withington[14], a jeweler from Janesville, Wisconsin, they were pulled by teams of horses in earlier years, but now by steam-powered tractors. It was one of these tractors that Charlie drove.

The United States entered World War I in April. The U. S. Army grew from 127,000[15] men to four times [16]that in the first year of the war. Before the war ended, more than 4.5 million men were in uniform[17]. This caused a widespread farm labor shortage at a time when farmers were urged to plant more food crops to meet wartime demand[18]. Charlie, however, was exempt from serving due to his earlier leg injury and being his family's sole bread winner.

Then, in the spring of 1918, the Flu Pandemic struck. Before it ended, there would be 50 million deaths [19]worldwide, with 650,000 [20]in the United States. Charlie's entire family had the flu at one time, including Lola. Neighbors had nowhere else to turn and struggled to help one another. Many doctors were off with the Army, and if it weren't for neighbors, the results might have been far worse. In every town and village, burials were a daily occurrence, sometimes as mass graves. As it was, Bud's illness soon turned into pneumonia, and he had to be hospitalized. He was just four and mortality for people younger than five years [21]old was high.

Chapter 8
On to Chicago

Some victims of influenza died within ten days of onset. Many died in only three. [22]Orin's (Buddy's) pneumonia was serious, requiring his admittance to the hospital in Springfield, where doctors had difficulty draining his lungs. At only four years old, and because of his small size, doctors had to remove a rib from his side in order to insert a tube to drain the fluid. Penicillin had yet to be discovered, and some doctors still treated patients by bloodletting.

Buddy had a very difficult time at first, but he eventually recovered as strong as before. Interestingly, the total bill for his hospital stay was just $16. As summer neared, each member of the family had fully recovered from their illnesses.

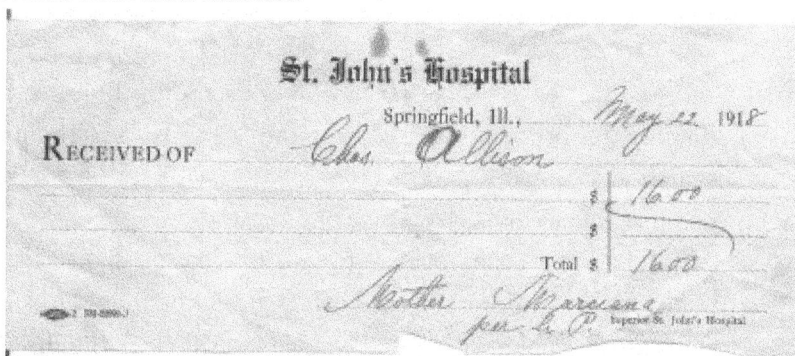

St. John's Hospital
Springfield, Ill., *May 22* 1918
RECEIVED OF *Chas. Allison*
$ *16.00*
$
Total $ *16.00*
Mother Marcene
per L.P. Superior St. John's Hospital

By the end of May, Bolton contacted Charlie to say it would be a little while yet, but his plans were unfolding. "Charlie," he said, "I got things rolling pretty good now. I'm making friends here and good connections. It's taking a while with all that's happened, but you better get up here pretty soon if you still want to be part of it."

Of course, Charlie did. He longed to be in Chicago, where there was greater opportunity, and now that opportunity appeared to be near at hand. So, in June, he moved his family, along with his friend, Shorty Knudson, to Chicago's north side.

With Bolton's help, Charlie got a job operating a cement mixer for Powers-Thompson Construction Company as they built roads in the area of Fox River Grove, Crystal Lake and Cary, north of Chicago.

Bolton had made a number of friends in Chicago and seemed to have influence in a wide range of businesses. A couple months later, Charlie was offered another job, this one at Anheuser-Busch. Once again, he repaired harnesses, but he also hauled beer. This arrangement worked well for Charlie and Lola for a couple of years.

During this time, Bolton introduced Charlie to Fred Goetz[23], who also went by "Van Ash" or "Von Ash," and variations such as "Vonesch" and "Van Ness."[24] His best-known alias would become Zeigler: "Shotgun George Zeigler[25]." Like Bolton, Goetz would be instrumental in Charlie's life, for the job with Anheuser-Busch would be brief, since Prohibition began soon after. With Prohibition, Anheuser Busch refitted their breweries to make ice cream[26]

The 18th Amendment forbade the "manufacture, sale and transportation of intoxicating liquors"—not their consumption. Anything "stashed away" prior was legal. Sacramental wine for religious purposes was allowed, as was "medicinal whiskey" sold in drug stores. With a physician's prescription, "patients" could legally buy a pint of hard liquor every ten days.

The government required companies to denature industrial alcohol to make it undrinkable by adding quinine, methyl alcohol and other toxic chemicals. This meant that bootleg liquor containing industrial alcohol had a foul taste and could possibly kill or leave a person blind, hence the term, "blind drunk."

As Charlie's job with Anheuser-Busch ended, Bolton came through again, supplying the money for a seventeen-room hotel for Charlie and Lola to operate. Charlie also opened what he called a "beanery," or soup kitchen, in a small building a few blocks away. It was little more than a tin shed. Folks were served simple meals there, mostly soups and sandwiches for the many of that era who could afford little more. He also served beer.

Charlie hired a man he had befriended, Pearl Robinson, to keep the place clean and to wash dishes. Pearl was unique in that, having had his legs amputated at the knees, he fastened shoes worn backward to the stumps of his legs.

While Charlie ran the soup kitchen, Lola managed the hotel, much as she had the boarding houses earlier. She also prepared some of the food, especially the soups, for the beanery.

On an afternoon in May of 1921, Bryan Bolton brought two acquaintances to the soup kitchen. One was Frank Nitti. The other Nick Greco. Bolton invited Charlie to talk business with Frank at one table while Nick took a seat at the counter. Nick was a sharp dresser in his fedora, brown business suit and tie and shiny brown wingtip shoes.

Lola noticed his eyes were deep brown too. She also noticed he was handsome and powerfully built. Nick laid his hat on the counter and asked for a cup of coffee. It being a hot day, Lola suggested he might be more comfortable if he removed his jacket.

"Oh, no, thanks. I'm fine as I am," he said, though clearly, he couldn't have been too comfortable. Beads of sweat peppered his brow.

Then Lola realized why he kept his coat on. Beneath his jacket she saw the butt of a pistol.

Casually, she asked, "You and Bryan been friends long?"

"Oh, we've known each other a while. I do small jobs for him sometimes."

"What do you do, if I can ask?"

"Collections," he said. "I travel quite a bit, here and there."

"Collections? Doesn't sound like a very pleasant job. Do you like it?"

"Pleasant? No. Can be exciting at times, and you get to see a lot of country."

"I see."

"Yeah, I got me a job to take care of here, and if it goes off without a hitch, I'll make a killin' and take a nice long vacation someplace."

"Hard for a married man to work like that, isn't it?" she asked.

"Yes, it was. My wife didn't like me being gone so much, so we split. I got me a boy and two girls, though I don't see much of them. But, Patti, that's my oldest, I see her two, three times a year. She's my favorite anyway."

The two carried on their conversation for a while longer before Lola had to go back to the kitchen. By then the men finished their discussion and, together with Nick, left.

Lola knew not to ask too much about the men's business, but her thoughts about Nick lingered.

Chapter 9

Arrested

A few weeks later, Charlie realized his relationship with Goetz was starting to pay off. Goetz helped make and distribute beer for "Papa Johnny" Torrio[27]. This was before Al Capone headed the organization and was merely a soldier for Torrio. Goetz convinced Charlie to sell Torrio's beer through his soup kitchen as well as liquor that he would help them make, Goetz providing all the supplies needed. Charlie agreed to the deal.

As promised, the materials for both the still and the liquor were delivered to the hotel through a coal chute. Charlie and Bolton immediately began building the still in the basement.

The setup was ingenious. Heat from cooking the mash vented through the chimney while copper pipes running alongside conducted the vapors to the attic where, through a series of copper coils, the alcohol was tapped off. This arrangement worked very well for over a year.

Then, while Charlie was at the soup kitchen, Shorty Knutson was tending the still when an explosion occurred. A fire began in the basement and quickly grew. He and Lola tried to control it, but there was no chance. Neighbors joined in to help save what they could.

Charlie, hearing about the fire, quickly rushed to help. But by the time he arrived, the hotel was completely engulfed in flames. All he could do was watch as the charred remains crumbled. There was little in the way of organized firefighting available for their neighborhood, and by the time firemen did arrive, all that remained standing was the chimney with its copper pipes alongside and the coils near the top waving like a flag. Charlie merely laughed at the spectacle. At least, he thought, he still had his soup kitchen.

But, as in any business, Charlie had competition there too. Most came from brothers, Bob and Elic White, who ran a place only two blocks away. The Whites, whose business had been suffering badly, made no secret about their enmity toward Charlie.

A few weeks after the fire, minor vandalism began occurring at Charlie's soup kitchen. First, a broken window, then a sliver of wood jammed into the door lock, then paint splashed on the outside and a bucket of grease poured at the entrance. Charlie suspected the Whites were responsible, but he had no proof.

And then, a more serious event happened. Two men entered Charlie's kitchen ordered a meal and a couple of beers. After being served, they revealed themselves to be revenuers. They arrested Charlie and everyone on his staff. The White brothers had tipped them off.

While Charlie sat in jail, officials questioned him about how he obtained his stock of beer, hoping his testimony would help them catch bigger fish. Charlie refused to talk. His refusal would hold him in good stead with Goetz.

Charlie was sentenced to three months in the county jail. While there, Lola had to operate the soup kitchen. Thankfully, daughter Goldie, then 13, was able to help by caring for young Bud.

Then, once again, Nick Greco appeared at the restaurant. Hanging his fedora on a peg on the wall, he sat at the counter. Lola noticed his brown business suit first. Since most customers wore the rough clothing of laborers or the destitute, she immediately recognized him.

"Nick?" she said. "What brings you here?"

"Lola," he said, by way of greeting. "Just stopped by for a cup of coffee, and to drop this off." He removed an envelope from his jacket. Laying it on the counter, he said, "Mr. Nitti asked me to bring this by. Just a little thank you for Charlie. He said to say he is very pleased with him."

"Well, I thank you, and thank mister, what'd you say his name was?"

"Nitti. Mr. Nitti wanted me to assure you not to worry about Charlie, that he would be all right, and that he'd be home before you know it."

"Well, thank Mr. Nitti for us and, should I open this?"

"If you like."

Taking a butter knife from beneath the counter, Lola slit the envelope and discovered four hundred-dollar bills inside. "Oh, my!" she exclaimed. She had never seen so much money at one time in her life. "What is all this for?"

Nick replied, "Appreciation. Mr. Nitti and the others appreciate good men, and Charlie's a good man. Now, if you'll excuse me, I have some other errands to run." Reaching for his hat, he nodded a farewell and left.

Hardly able to contain herself, Lola retreated to the kitchen to look again at the money. Having never seen a hundred-dollar bill before, she ached to show them to Charlie, although he wasn't released from jail until the spring of 1922.

Just prior to Charlie's release, another fire struck. This one was suspicious, for it started at night in an alley behind the building. The fire gutted his soup kitchen. The tin shed was destroyed. Charlie was sure his competitors, Bob and Elic White were responsible. And in a short while he learned he was right. They had hired a pair of men to do the job.

Things were starting to heat up in Chicago.

Chapter 10
The Organization

After Charlie's release from jail, he and Lola were invited to northern Wisconsin to the retreat of Fred Goetz and his girlfriend, Irene Dorsey[28]. There, Charlie learned that Fred and Irene had met at her family's diner[29] in Wilmington, Illinois. He also learned more about his friend Bryan Bolton and that Fred had known him years earlier. The two had grown up in central Illinois and ran separate bootlegging operations near Springfield and East St. Louis until Goetz moved to Chicago to work for the "Organization."

And organized it was. Giovanni "Papa Johnny" Torrio led the South Side Gang[30], and Al Capone was his right-hand man. They had divided the organization into branches: Administration Operations and Enforcement. Jake Guzik was in Administration, while Frank Nitti, a recent addition, was in charge of Operations. Tony "Joe

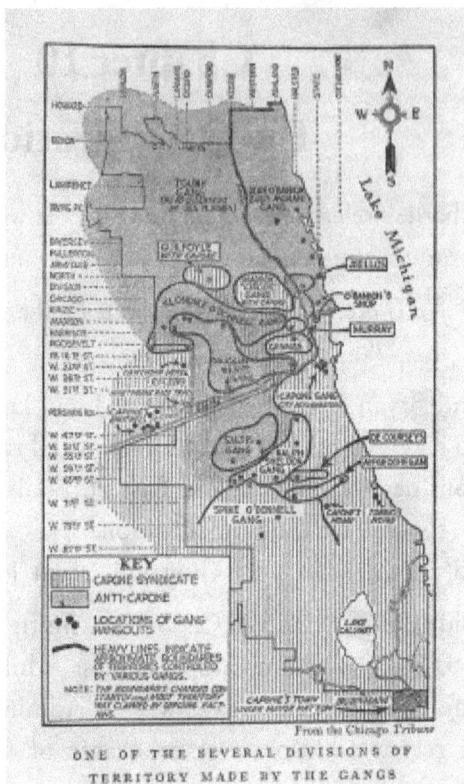

From the Chicago Tribune

ONE OF THE SEVERAL DIVISIONS OF
TERRITORY MADE BY THE GANGS

Batters" Accardo headed Enforcement. Goetz was brought in from the affiliated Karpis-Barker Gang for his business sense and his supposedly similar values.

While the Karpis-Barker Gang dealt with bank robberies and kidnappings, Torrio wanted nothing to do with such crimes. He, as well as Capone, favored "victimless" crimes[31]: booze, prostitution, and gaming. This was a business decision, for violence could turn the community against them and incite the police to greater efforts. However, dealing with competition was another matter and harsher tactics were sometimes needed. Here is where Goetz' business philosophy would eventually run counter to Torrio's.

One might view a gang much like a government: Politics and economics were involved in every move, and loyalty was demanded. A man took sides and didn't switch – unless there was much to gain – for doing so could cost him his life. Some, of course, did switch, because ambitious men knew which way the wind blew and were sometimes more loyal to money and power.

Torrio knew it was necessary to talk, even to one's enemies. But doing so could be like dealing with a spider or praying mantis; one mistake could cost your life. Yet, negotiations were a regular part of doing business. That is why gang leaders were always tough. You had to be tough to survive. And even then, life might be short.

Torrio met with all the major Chicago bootleggers to work out a system of territories[32]. While Dean O'Banion, who worked behind his cover as a floral shop owner, controlled most of Chicago's north side, Claude "Screwy" Maddox and his Circus Cafe Gang was the only North Side organization allied with Torrio aside from Martin Guilfoyle. Guilfoyle and his partners ran games behind his cigar store and a beer business from an office. The O'Donnell gang, three brothers, had the west side. Angelo Genna's gang was in the middle and allied with Torrio. These and others eventually united against the North Side Gang.

Charlie wasn't privy to these details, but he now had an "in" with Goetz and Torrio's organization. Yet he was only a very small part of the whole.

Charlie knew these were tough men, men who played the game hard and played for keeps. He learned, too, that Bob and Elic White, Charlie's earlier soup kitchen adversaries, had been supplied by O'Banion, the main rival of Johnny Torrio and Al Capone, and that it was men from O'Banion's North Side Gang[33] who had torched Charlie's soup kitchen. Charlie recognized this as the beginning of a challenge for territory, and he knew the war was just beginning.

Yet, the time spent at Goetz's retreat was devoted to relaxation, fishing mostly. The two couples talked casually about many things while Goetz shared his ideas of what he might eventually do with his retreat. Goetz enjoyed being away from the city and its demands and dreamt of someday getting away from all of it.

Charlie, too, was feeling the pull of this big country, the wildness and freedom it offered. After so many years of yearning for city life, he was beginning to feel the attraction of the lakes and forest and the quiet.

The two men talked about what the retreat could become and how to make it happen. Charlie said, "You've seen how the folks around here live; they got little more than shacks. They're tough men, timber cutters, farmers scratching out a living in rocky soil. I don't know how they manage, but by Christ, they do. And I'll bet there's enough men here with backbone and knowhow to put up whatever you want to build."

"Charlie," Goetz said, "I'll bet you're right about that. And maybe we'll have a chance to find that out."

This was the first of several trips Charlie and Lola made to Goetz's retreat. Goetz's ideas developed along with their friendship. And it was that friendship that eventually provided Charlie an opportunity to move once more.

Chapter 11

Gang War

After returning to Chicago, Charlie found things heating up. It was the spring of 1924. Recently appointed Director of the Federal Bureau of Investigation, J. Edgar Hoover's personal desire was combating communism[34], yet many changes he implemented placed pressure on gang activity all across the country. Nowhere was that pressure felt more than in Chicago.

The FBI estimated that Chicago alone had 1,300 gangs, large and small, by the mid-1920s[35], a situation that led to turf wars and other violence between rival gangs.

With raids and arrests soaring among gangs, the resulting fear and instability lent impetus for gang members to break loyalties and challenge leaderships. There had always been incentive to crowd into or take over the territory of others. This unrest persuaded many that now was the time to act.

As a result, the Genna syndicate[36], allied with Torrio, sought to move into O'Banion's North Chicago territory.[37]

Realizing the bloodshed that might result, O'Banion reminded Torrio of their agreement to divide the territories. He asked Torrio to stop the Gennas. Torrio refused. In retaliation, O'Banion began hijacking shipments of alcohol belonging to the Genna brothers[38]

The Genna brothers were outraged by this and wanted to retaliate by killing O'Banion. Mike Merlo[39], an underworld power broker, vetoed the killing. But when Merlo died of an illness a short time later and Torrio discovered that O'Banion had cheated him out of $500,000 in a brewery acquisition deal, Torrio lost his patience and ordered O'Banion killed himself.

Torrio's men - Frankie Yale, John Scalise, and Albert Anselmi, with Mike Genna representing the six Genna brothers - arrived at O'Banion's flower shop[40], supposedly to buy floral tributes for Merlo's funeral. Yale and O'Banion shook hands, with Yale grasping O'Banion's hand tightly. At that point, Scalise and Anselmi quickly fired bullets into O'Banion's chest and throat[41]. Yale then fired a final shot into the back of O'Banion's head.

This was the spark that set off a full-scale war among the gangs.

Hymie Weiss[42] then assumed leadership[43] of the North Side Gang, initiating a string of retaliatory attacks against Torrio. They began by ambushing Torrio's man, Al Capone. Shooting into his car, they failed to kill him but left him shaken.

Days later, three men, including Bugs Moran and Vincent Drucci, attempted to assassinate Torrio[44] as he was driving his car while shopping with his wife. Torrio was shot in the jaw, lungs, groin, legs, and abdomen. Moran attempted to deliver the coup de grâce into Torrio's head but was out of ammunition. Drucci urgently signaled that there was no time to reload, and the North Siders quickly left. Though severely wounded, Torrio survived. Police caught those they thought were the shooters and brought them to Torrio's hospital bedside, but he refused to name them.

After recovering, Torrio gave total control of the Outfit to Capone[45] saying, "It's all yours, Al. Me? I'm quitting." He then moved back to Italy, walking away from an organization that was netting nearly $70 million[46] a year in 1920s dollars.

Suppliers for the Chicago Outfit lay scattered across the Midwest, and Nitti, in charge of Operations, offered Charlie an opportunity to operate a still near Springfield, getting away from the action. Charlie jumped at the chance. Earlier, he had wanted to be in the big city for the opportunities offered there, and now he had an opportunity to get out.

"By Jesus," said Charlie, "I'd have to be crazy not to."

With that, they shook hands and Charlie made the move.

Charlie was beginning to realize more fully the wide reach the Chicago Outfit had. The Organization depended on folks in small towns and farm communities to produce small batches of one to five gallons of "bathtub gin" per week in their homes. They were paid [47]fifty to seventy-five cents per gallon, while that gallon sold for perhaps $6 in Chicago, a tidy profit.

Charlie's task was to act as a "funnel," directing deliveries from individual producers to his warehouse, then shipping the alcohol to Chicago where it would be further processed, for few could tolerate the bad taste of this "bathtub gin[48]," which may have been produced from fermented "mash" made from corn sugar, fruit, beets, or even potato peels. Often it was mixed with glycerin and juniper oil to "enhance" its taste. Charlie often received it as 200-proof alcohol, which was then watered down to 100-proof or less.

This truly was a business that provided jobs and income for many people. It was the sort of organization Torrio had always wanted to develop, one seen and felt as beneficial to the average citizen. Now, with Capone at the helm, that strategy continued.

Running this, one of the newer operations, Charlie was close to where he had grown up, and benefited from connections originally established by Bolton. Those connections made access to sources easier. Still, it was a year before the operation produced more than 100 gallons a week.

Then trouble developed. Hoover's FBI was pursuing bootleggers on many fronts, and finally found Charlie's operation. He was arrested.

While he sat in jail, the FBI pressed Charlie for information once again. And again, he resisted. Months later, upon his release, Goetz rewarded Charlie for his loyalty with an offer he could not refuse: a move to northern Wisconsin as caretaker of his retreat.

Goetz had said he might someday get a chance to see if those Wisconsin backwoodsmen could build his dream retreat. He would soon find out.

Chapter 12
The Move North

Charlie eagerly shared with Lola his opportunity to move to northern Wisconsin. Both were happy to get away from the pressures of running an operation, and they hesitated to return to Chicago, especially with its mounting danger.

In making his move to Goetz's retreat, Charlie's first task was to assess the materials at hand: trees for felling, rock for walls and foundations and such, and then to line up laborers. He and Goetz had discussed the plan thoroughly. Since the lodge, the main building, had been completed, Charlie was to erect other buildings: a guest house, garage, storage, gazebo, icehouse, an entryway onto the property, and a pier extending far out into the 37-acre lake. This was a huge undertaking for a man with relatively little education. He knew success depended on finding capable workers.

Charlie led the way north in the fall of 1927, taking young Bud with him. Lola and Goldie were to follow in the spring. Bud, about to turn 14, stood a slender five feet four inches tall, topped with an unruly mop of red-orange hair. Like his father, he had limited education, yet was a natural at mathematics and all things mechanical. And Bud was strong and wiry, a hard worker, and quick to learn. He would prove to be a great asset to his father.

After loading Charlie's 1920 Ford Model-T with food, clothing, and tools, Charlie and Bud set out for Wisconsin's north woods. They shared the driving, as Wisconsin had no age restrictions or license requirements at the time. Few roads were paved, so they rarely reached speeds as high as 40 miles per hour. With fueling stations far apart, especially in the north, and none open after 9 p.m., Charlie and Bud had to pull to the side of the road and sleep in the car, making the 450-mile trip take two days.

Upon arrival, Charlie began to realize how much work he was facing.

"Holy bald-headed Jesus, boy, there's enough to do here to kill a dozen mules. You think we're up to it?"

"Good as done, Pa," replied Bud, who shared his father's "can do" attitude.

"Good as done, eh? Well, let's get to it then."

After unloading the car and settling into the lodge, Charlie spent the next few days assessing what materials were at hand and exploring the surrounding forest. He took stock of the trees they might use and discovered massive stumps left from the timber harvest of 50 years earlier[49]. Still, there was plenty of second-growth cedar and white pine, as well as hemlock, basswood, oak, and birch, to meet his needs

Leaving Bud to cut firewood for the winter, Charlie drove to Couderay, the nearest village, six miles away. There he put word out that he would be hiring men in the spring. The news spread quickly.

Soil in that part of Wisconsin was very poor, making crop farming uncertain at best. Consequently, most men depended on timber for their livelihood, working either in sawmills or as independent sawyers. And because harvesting timber was a winter activity, men struggled to make ends meet after the logging season. But Charlie was offering cash, which was hard to come by for many, so in just a few weeks, he interviewed and selected the men he would need in the spring.

Meanwhile, Charlie and Bud turned to the task of cutting timber from the surrounding forest. The cold of winter allowed logs to dry sufficiently for use once the weather warmed. As for firewood, the slash trimmings would do nicely. And once the snow began to fall, it fell in abundance, easing the task of skidding logs.

It was in the deep snow and rutted roads that Charlie's Model-T proved its worth. Its narrow tires and high clearance provided transportation when others had to rely on horses. Even with its small 20-horsepower engine, it was able to drag many of the logs they cut.

Still, Charlie often hired a team of horses from a local farmer, Jozef Chernyak, who was too old to cut timber, but could drive his horses. Together, the three of them cut, hauled, and stacked the logs needed to build the caretaker's cottage and more, so that, when spring arrived, the logs would be ready for use.

Lola and Goldie arrived early in the spring of 1928, and immediately set about cleaning the retreat's lodge. Both women were lean and strong, near equals to the men in their ability to work hard. Their strong backs were great assets for collecting fieldstone, so abundant on the property, for the foundation.

Once enough rock was gathered, Charlie and Bud mixed mortar and laid the foundation. As they prepared the logs, Chernyak brought lumber and supplies from the village for the windows and roof. With Chernyak's help, the caretaker's home was completed in a matter of weeks. For Charlie, it was looking like his first real home.

By early June, Goetz arrived. He was there not only to observe the progress on his retreat, but to escape the city, where things were truly heating up.

Chapter 13
The Hideout

Goetz's arrival was unexpected but not surprising. A letter from him, inquiring about progress, suggested that Charlie had left at a good time. In the letter, Charlie learned of a Capone associate, "Jackie" Adler, being kidnapped[50] by the South Side O'Donnell's gang. But, because he was released unharmed, Charlie thought little more of it. He believed the greatest dangers were to those more directly involved in the operation.

But later he learned Capone's restaurant manager at the Hawthorne Inn, Ted Anton[51], was kidnapped and killed[52] by the North Side Gang. Charlie was then more appreciative of Goetz's offer to come north, since Charlie had been managing the Sangamon County operation.

While working at the retreat, fresh rumors told of events in Chicago, but Charlie failed to fully understand just how bad things were until Goetz arrived.

"Good thing you came up here when you did, Charlie," he said. "It's a lot healthier. I needed to get away for a while myself."

"Glad you're here. Going to be with us for a while?" Charlie asked.

"Wish I could."

"Why can't you?"

"Business. Got things lined up that need to be done," was all he said, never hinting at the job that awaited him. [53][*Goetz, also known as "Shotgun" Ziegler, was one of five men who killed Frankie Yale weeks later in New York City on Sunday, July 1, 1928*]

Over the next few days, Goetz worked alongside Charlie and the others, discussing more ideas for his retreat. He also shared news with Charlie of several "hits" attempted against Capone by the Aiello brothers.[54] [55]Fortunately, Capone had been alerted each time. In two incidents, the hitmen, Sam Valante and New York gangster Antonio Torchio, were killed as soon as they arrived in Chicago[56].

Goetz smiled as he told Charlie about it. "Al's got some good eyes looking out for him," he said, adding, "they put a halt to those guys, especially that bastard Torchio."

He shared with Charlie how Joe Aiello and Capone began feuding after Antonio Lombardo[57] was named head of the Unione Siciliana[58], a Sicilian-American benevolent society. Aiello wanted that position and believed Capone was responsible for Lombardo's election.

Angered, Aiello became an ally of Dean O'Banion[59] and other Capone enemies. Together, they organized machine-gun ambushes against Lombardo and Capone, one directly across from Lombardo's home[60], and another at a cigar store frequented by Capone. Fortunately, both attempts failed, but it ended the peace agreement in force since the murder of Capone's rival, Hymie Weiss[61].

Goetz neglected to tell Charlie about other events, such as Chicago saloon owner and distributor for the Sheldon Gang, John Costanaro, being killed.[62] Nor about John "Mitters" Foley's murder while driving through South Side O'Donnell's territory[63]. In retaliation for Foley's murder, gunmen Charles "Big Hayes" Hubacek and Frank "Lefty" Koncil were killed. So numerous became the killings and retaliatory acts that many of the crime family members went into hiding. Thus, Goetz's unannounced visit to his retreat.

One evening, at dinner, Goetz told Charlie that he believed it important for Bud to complete his education. He proposed sending him to high school in Rice Lake.

"How can we do that?" Charlie asked.

"By train," Goetz answered. "He can leave from Couderay and spend the week in Rice Lake, then come back on the weekends. I'll pay his way, room and board. He needs it. And I think he's worth it. I've seen that boy work. What d'you say?"

"By God," Charlie said, "I think that's a great idea. He can't live here in these woods all his life. Let's do it." And so, it was decided.

After another two weeks, satisfied with the progress being made, Goetz returned to Chicago. It was near the end of June. The dangers there were no less, but he had other jobs to do[64], especially one that would briefly take him to New York. He was, after all, a businessman.

Charlie and Bud still had tasks to complete. They began work on the garage, one large enough to accommodate a half dozen cars or more. For this, they hired other men from the area, and within a week the foundation was completed. In another week, the building was finished. Charlie had indeed found men who knew how to work.

By late August, they added an icehouse with walls a foot thick and a floor two feet below ground level, a building suitable to hold enough ice to last through summer.

Charlie said, "We'll have a helluva time filling this bastard with ice. It'll take half the ice in the lake. And gettin' it up here will be a bitch."

"I won't be able to help ya wid dat," Chernyak said. "I won't put my horses on da ice. But my boy, Stefan, he got him a contraption to skid logs wid. Not so fast as da horses, but it'll get da chob done. I'll haff him come oer when da time comes."

Then they turned to the property entrance. Charlie's first challenge was to improve the dirt track that had served for a driveway, so he hired men with the equipment necessary to do the job.

While the road was being graded and graveled, he and the others erected an arched entryway of stone and wood beams near the road, an impressive sight to folks in that area.

Chernyak and the women loosened fieldstones from the ground and, heavy though the work was, loaded them onto a stoneboat for the horses to drag to the entrance. While they did this, Charlie and the men mixed mortar and erected pillars and the archway. It was mid-September before the entrance and driveway were finished.

With fall fast approaching, several projects were yet to be completed before freeze-up. It was also time for Bud to leave for school.

The Rice Lake, Dallas & Menomonie Railway[65] had once served a sawmill near Eddy Creek, just outside Couderay. The sawmill was no more, but the rail line still served the village and nearby Indian reservation, supplying transportation to Rice Lake, 40 miles south. So, with his room and board arranged, and a couple dollars in his pocket, Bud left for high school.

Although it had been a busy summer, one in which Charlie had proven his ability to get things done, he still had another task on his agenda, a gazebo overlooking the lake. This was something Goetz looked forward to for the view it would offer across the shining lake toward a nearly pristine forest. The pier would jut far out into the lake, providing a place to moor boats or for guests to fish from – possibly even a place to tie up a float plane.

Chapter 14
Visitors

While most days were pleasant in early October, the weather could be unpredictable, so Charlie was anxious to begin work on the gazebo. The site overlooking the lake was very rocky and too difficult to sink posts into, so, once again they used local stone for the foundation. This resulted in an attractive and solid structure.

Once that task was completed, they started on the pier. Charlie and his crew cut down many of the small trees lining the shore for this. Doing so, not only enhanced the view but provided cedar posts for the pilings needed. When finished, the pier extended nearly a hundred feet, out to where the water finally reached a depth of six feet. This task took two weeks to complete, with cold and rain making a hard job worse.

Days after the pier was finished, a letter arrived from Goetz. In it he wrote that he would arrive that weekend, accompanied by "a number of guests." Charlie was to stock provisions enough for as many as twenty people, some of them women.

This was a tall order, but calling on Lola's experience, gained through supplying items for their boarding house and the beanery, they soon compiled a list of goods too vast to be filled in the nearby village. Charlie had to drive to Hayward to get everything they needed. Lola insisted she would need help in handling the extra housekeeping chores and proposed that Charlie hire an Indian woman Lola had befriended, Julia Corbine, for this job. Charlie agreed and hired her.

Shortly after they finished stocking supplies, Goetz arrived, along with his wife, Irene. Goetz looked around at what had been accomplished. He was pleased. He especially liked the gazebo view overlooking the lake as a sunset cast its glow on the forest beyond.

"Beautiful job, Charlie. I'm impressed. I hope the others like it. We're going to put the married couples in the bedrooms upstairs. The rest will have to make do best they can. And just so you know, I've arranged it with the Outfit to provide regular compensation for you. You're one of us now."

This was wonderful news to Charlie, especially because so many people were badly hurt by the Depression. His loyalty was paying off.

Bryan Bolton[66] arrived later that evening with his wife, Veva. Over the course of the next two days, other guests arrived. Among them[67]were Al Capone and his entourage of protectors, including Louis Campagna with his wife, Charlotte, along with Fred "Killer" Burke[68]/[69].Then came Frank Nitti[70] with his new bride, Anna[71]. Gus Winkler[72] arrived the next day with Jack McGurn. Finally, the corpulent Illinois Sen.[73] Daniel Serritella and his wife Rose arrived, together with Chicago 20th Ward[74]Alderman William Pacelli. This was, indeed, a large group to accommodate at the lodge, but everyone seemed to enjoy the camaraderie and soon settled in.

Goetz introduced Charlie and Lola to the guests as they arrived, instructing Charlie to make sure everyone was comfortable and had something to do.

It was then that Bud returned from Rice Lake, having been away at school. He hadn't been back to the retreat in more than four weeks. Asked about school, he shrugged his shoulders and admitted he hadn't gone but a couple of days. Instead, he met some other young men and spent nearly all of his time shooting pool with them.

"You what?" Charlie exploded.

"But, Pa," Bud argued, "they weren't teaching me anything I didn't already know."

"Well, that's it then. We're not sending you off to play pool. Your school days are over."

And so, Bud's education ended in the eighth grade, though he never stopped learning.

That evening, after dinner, Goetz and his guests sat around the vast fireplace enjoying its warmth and discussing how they might spend their time. Rafts of migrating ducks had settled on the lake, filling the air with the cacophony of their squabbling. Hearing this, some of the men expressed an interest in hunting.

"Charlie," Goetz said, "can you arrange for these fellows to do some duck hunting?"

"Sure can, and I know just the guys for it.

With that, Charlie told Bud, "Here's what you're going to do. You're going to the village tomorrow and arrange for some of the local guys to come out here as guides. Get Frank Crandall for the duck hunters and see if Eddie Anderson will take some folks fishing too. You can do that, can't you?"

"Sure, Pa."

Arrangements were made, and the hunt was on.

Chapter 15
The Hunt

That following morning, Frank Crandall arrived to meet the men he was to guide. After introductions were made, Frank made sure each had the proper gun and ammunition. Finding them well prepared, he instructed them to be ready by 4 o'clock the following morning.

"I'll have a couple of boats at the pier. I'm heading across the lake now to set up some blinds for you. You guys better dress warm; it's going to be cold tomorrow. I'll see you in the morning."

After Frank left, several of the guests, including the women, went down to fish from the pier. Capone remained in the kitchen intent on fixing supper for everyone. That's when Charlie learned Capone loved to cook and took great pride in his culinary skills.

Lola volunteered to help. Capone asked her to scald tomatoes while he fairly danced about the kitchen, chopping onions and garlic, dropping them into a large pot with hot olive oil, then adding oregano. As these ingredients simmered, he squeezed tomatoes by hand, adding them to the oil and herbs.

As he did this, he broke into song, surprising Lola, who was kneading dough and baking bread. She was fascinated by how playful and relaxed he was in the kitchen as he tended the sauce and talked about family and growing up in Brooklyn. Lola found him to be a very charming person.

As the sauce simmered, he tasted it, adding salt, pepper and then basil, sharing with Lola that basil should never be added too early lest its flavor be lost. One other thing, he suggested, "At the end, you wanta put in some butter. This'll make the sauce smooth, and it'll stick to your pasta better."

The two of them remained in the kitchen throughout the afternoon, sharing recipes and tales.

Returning from fishing, Charlie entered the lodge and was met by the aroma of tomato sauce cooking and seeing Capone standing at the woodstove. Smiling at Charlie, Capone said, "Smells good, don't it? Betcha didn't know I was such a cook. It's my ma's recipe."

"By God, that smells good," Charlie admitted.

Others drifted in as darkness fell, the aroma of Capone's tomato sauce blending with that of Lola's freshly baked bread. The atmosphere was perfect for laughter and talk, although it eventually shifted from the gaiety of the day to more grave subjects. Charlie then realized that these men were here, not only to relax, but to deal with serious matters too.

That next morning, promptly at 4, Frank rapped on the door, ready to take the men duck hunting. Lola and Julia had prepared sandwiches for the men who strolled quietly to the boats in the predawn darkness.

Throughout the morning, shots were heard as ducks continued to drift in from the north. Cold weather was sure to follow.

Before noon, the men returned with ducks and stories to tell, filling the lodge with laughter. Charlie hung the ducks in the garage to be cleaned days later, as was the practice at that time. Allowing game birds, ducks in particular, to age for several days before cleaning, made the meat tender.

Eddie Anderson appeared shortly after lunch, prepared to guide any who wanted to fish for muskies. A 51-pounder had been caught a few years earlier from Chief Lake, just ten miles away. This enthused a few of the men, although the rest were satisfied fishing from the pier or from shore.

Each day was the same, fishing, hunting and relaxing, while each night, Goetz, Capone, Nitti, Bolton and the others set aside time for more serious discussion[75]. What this was about, Charlie did not know at the time, only that the mood afterward was very somber.

In late October, a hard freeze hit the area, and by the first weeks of November, several inches of snow had accumulated, brightening the mood considerably. Charlie suggested the men might like to try hunting deer. This galvanized the men into the spirit of hunting again, so

Charlie directed Bud to drive to Couderay and organize some men to drive deer for the hunters.

That next afternoon Bud stationed the hunters, spreading them apart on ridges where they had a better field of view, while Charlie organized the drivers to advance toward them from some distance away. Bud had placed Capone on a particularly advantageous site and stayed nearby to assist him or any other shooter who might be successful. Capone, rather than using a rifle, carried a brace of long-barrel handguns.

Once everyone was in place, the drive began. Soon, gunshots echoed through the woods. For the next couple hours, the hunters fired at passing deer, killing three. Capone, cold and unable to stand quietly, never saw a deer.

That night, Bud related to his father what he had seen. "You shoulda seen 'em Pa. He pulled a big ole pistol outta his coat and stood there waitin', then tucked it in his pocket and blew on his hands. He was cold. Next thing I knew, he was stompin' his feet and swingin's his arms, trying to keep warm. Hell, he musta scared off every deer for half a mile."

By the end of the week, the hunters had killed several deer, and after giving most of the meat to locals, a feast was in order.

Later, Lola said, about what was heard and read in newspapers about Capone, "I don't believe all that stuff they say about him. He's just like any other businessman you might meet. Very pleasant. And generous too. Look what he gave us. And he gave all that meat away to folks too. Such a nice man."

But it was time to return to Chicago. It was the end of November. Before leaving, Capone's men were instructed to take Lola and Velma (Goldie) shopping in Hayward where they were each bought fur coats. Then, upon leaving, Charlie was presented a set of shotguns, Winchester Model 12's, one in 16, the other in 20 gauge, while Bud was given a pump action .22; a Winchester Model 90.

It was a busy and productive visit. Although Charlie had no idea what the late-night discussions had been about, the entire country was about to witness the shocking results of them.

Chapter 16
Valentine's Day Murders

By mid-winter, Charlie and Bud were busily cutting ice from the lake and hauling it to the icehouse. And, true to his word, Chernyak's son Stefan arrived with his log skidder – a tracked device powered by a gasoline engine. Noisy and slow, it was a steady puller that helped them complete the task within a week.

The men packed hundreds of pounds of ice beneath mounds of sawdust that had been gathered from the various building projects or brought from nearby lumber mills. Meanwhile, in Chicago, another kind of job was underway.

Hymie Weiss, head of the North Side gang, and his second-in-command, Bugs Moran, had been a challenge to Capone's South Side Gang. Earlier[76], they had attempted to kill Johnny Torrio and Capone, with Torrio being badly injured. In retaliation, Weiss was killed by Capone's gang, and Bugs Moran took over as head of the North Side gang.

After repeated attempts to kill one another, including one with Moran's men firing nearly a thousand rounds into the Hawthorne Inn[77], Capone's headquarters, Capone decided on the meeting just completed at Goetz's lodge.

These plans were now being turned into action. With Capone's deep hatred for Moran, he wanted to eliminate him and his gang once and for all.

The plan called for some men to offer Moran a load of hijacked Canadian whiskey, available for a cheap price. It would be delivered to him at S.M.C. Cartage Company on North Clark Street. This was where Moran kept his bootlegging trucks. Moran accepted the offer.

Bolton[78]/[79] and Jimmy "Swede" Morand kept watch from a rented room cross the street, ready to alert the others when Moran appeared. Seeing who they believed was Moran with several others, Goetz and Fred "Killer" Burke, disguised as police officers moved in with two other men.

The result, on February 14, 1929, was the St. Valentine's Day Massacre; seven men killed. When police arrived, they found Frank Gusenberg still alive with 14 bullet wounds.

Asking him who did it, he replied, " I ain't no copper. Nobody shot me[80]." He died three hours later.

The intended target, Bugs Moran, was missed. He was late in arriving.

And Capone? He was conveniently vacationing in Florida.

Moran lost so many important men that he could no longer control his territory, so while Capone failed to kill him[81], he did succeed in destroying his organization.

Capone never returned to Goetz's retreat in Couderay, and Charlie lost track of Goetz, unaware that he had begun his own bootlegging operations in Kansas.

Chapter 17
Fast Eddie

It was some time before Charlie learned of the events in Chicago. But with the visitors gone and the task of cutting and storing ice complete, he had time to do as he pleased, and he was pleased to hunt deer. He hunted, not only for himself, but to help supply his neighbors with venison. Deer were not abundant in Wisconsin at the time, and hunting seasons were open only on alternate years, being closed on odd years. This was an odd year, 1929. But that didn't stop people from being hungry, or from hunting.

There was a growing market for illegal venison in the cities, and Charlie regularly furnished customers in the Twin Cities of Minneapolis and Saint Paul. It was a lucrative market and, not unlike the bootlegging trade, competition could be fierce.

Bud enjoyed hunting too, and he was good at it. Although only 15, he was at home in the woods. One February day, while carrying the .22 given to him by Capone, he killed a deer and had just begun dragging it out of the woods when he was approached by a game warden.

"You know there's no open season on deer, don't you?" the warden asked.

"We're hungry," was Bud's reply.

Fully aware of the difficulties faced by so many in that area, the warden, scolded Bud for killing deer out of season. Then, after making him promise he wouldn't hunt any more, he let him take the deer. The warden didn't know that Bud and his father already had several others hanging in the garage.

A later incident involving deer occurred when Charlie met an acquaintance in the village. The man asked, "Charlie, I need some meat. You got any?"

Charlie said, "Sure, I got meat. There's thirteen deer hanging in my garage now. Take what you need."

That afternoon, when Charlie returned to the retreat, he found the man had removed the hind quarters from all thirteen deer.

"That son-of-a-bitch!" he said. "If I ever see him again, I'll have his hind quarters."

While it would be more than a year before Charlie would see the man again, as time passed, so did much of Charlie's anger. And when they finally met up in a tavern in the village, the incident was recalled in a boisterous manner with loud insults and laugher.

Capone received a subpoena to appear before a federal grand jury in Chicago on March 12, 1929, for violations of the Prohibition Act. His lawyers filed for postponement attesting that Capone had been ill and confined to bed. But the U.S. Attorney's Office had obtained statements that Capone attended racetracks in the Miami area and a cruise to Nassau, and he appeared in good health on each occasion.

Thus, compelled to attend or be jailed, he appeared. Upon completion of his testimony, Capone was then arrested for contempt of court. Posting bond, he was released.

Just two months later, he and his bodyguard were arrested [82] in Philadelphia for carrying concealed weapons. Sentenced to terms of one year each, Capone served his time and was released in nine months for good behavior on March 17, 1930.

While Capone was in prison, the stock market crash occurred in the fall of 1929, setting off the Great Depression. During his time in prison and throughout the Depression, Capone continued to donate[83] money to charity and open soup kitchens[84]. Ordinary folks saw him and those like him as champions of individualism; self-made men surviving in tough economic times. Many saw him as Lola had said, "...just like any other businessman you might meet. Very pleasant. And generous too."

Charlie had heard nothing of Goetz' whereabouts. He had no idea that, on November 7, 1929, while armed with machineguns, Goetz, Gus Winkler and four others, made off with over $350,000[85] in cash and securities from the Farmers and Merchants Bank in Jefferson, Wisconsin. It was the largest haul in the state's history at that time.

Neither had Charlie heard of another man who, in two more years, would become a major player in his life, "Easy Edward J. O'Hare[86], also known as "Fast Eddie."

Chapter 18

A New Boss

Edward J. O'Hare was a lawyer from St. Louis who enjoyed wealth and was not afraid to step on toes to achieve it. He had discovered that defending criminals was profitable, not only through high fees, but by gaining tips about other means of making money. O'Hare fit right in with those he defended.

He had been attorney for Owen P. Smith, developer of the mechanical rabbit used in dog racing. When Smith died in 1927, O'Hare cheated Smith's wife out of any rights she had to the invention and gained control for himself. He then moved to Chicago, where Capone took an immediate liking to him and brought him into the Hawthorne Kennel Club, a Cicero dog racetrack, as a major partner.

O'Hare had recently divorced his wife, Selma. Together, they had three children. Daughters Patricia, 12, and Marilyn, 7, lived with their mother in St. Louis. He also had a son, Eddie "Butch" O'Hare, the same age as Bud, who was then 17. But unlike Bud, did little but loaf about. Because of his laziness, the elder O'Hare enrolled him at Western Military Academy in Alton, Illinois. The senior O'Hare desperately wanted his son to become something

URSULA SUE GRANATA

better, and in time, that desire would be fulfilled[87].

By 1931, O'Hare became the racetrack's president, gaining power and influence through his Capone ties. He also found himself infatuated with a beautiful woman who worked as a receptionist and secretary at the track, Ursula Sue Granata[88]. She was the daughter of Congressman, Peter C. Granata. But Ursula was a good Catholic, and the Church wouldn't recognize O'Hare's divorce, so they were unable to marry. O'Hare hoped the Vatican would grant a request for dispensation.

Marriage was also in the making for Charlie's daughter. Then 21, Velma had moved to Milwaukee to study. There she met and married a young contractor, Perry Apfel. Perry worked for his father's contracting business but desired to be on his own, and when the time was right, he would.

O'Hare, meanwhile, unhappy working for Capone, wanted to be free of the Outfit. Knowing Capone was being investigated for tax evasion, O'Hare was certain that he would be charged next. Hoping for a chance to save himself from prison[89] and start a new life with Ursala, he secretly turned against Capone by asking a reporter, John Rogers, to arrange a meeting with IRS agent Frank J. Wilson[90]. Wilson later said: "On the inside of the gang, I had one of the best undercover men I have ever known: Eddie O'Hare."

The Outfit was unaware that O'Hare was talking to the feds, enabling him to learn that Capone had rigged the jury[91]. O'Hare alerted the government, and the jury was switched with another before the trial began. As a result, Capone was convicted. Sentenced[92] to eleven years in federal prison. For his cooperation[93], O'Hare was a free man.

Now O'Hare could start anew. In April of 1932, he bought Goetz's 407-acre retreat through the Federal Acceptance Corporation of St. Paul, of which he was trustee. Three months later, he had ownership transferred to his own name, and Charlie was about to meet his new boss.

Chapter 19
Days of Change

After buying the retreat in 1932, the senior O'Hare arrived unexpectedly on a spring afternoon. Introducing himself as the new owner, he told Charlie what was expected of him, adding, in no uncertain terms, that no one was allowed on the property aside from Charlie's family and whatever workmen might be required.

Having spent a few days looking over his newly acquired property, O'Hare returned to Chicago, leaving Charlie with a clear impression that he would be a harsh and demanding man, a man totally unlike Goetz. Their relationship was to be distant, at best. But for now, Charlie's job seemed secure.

Charlie continued his role as caretaker, maintaining the buildings and grounds, yet he had plenty of time to enjoy the freedom he had found in Wisconsin's north country. Good fishing and hunting abounded in the wilds. Peace and solitude surrounded him, no matter that the rest of the country was still suffering from the Great Depression.

O'Hare made several more visits to his retreat, each time unannounced. The relationship between him and Charlie remained cool. O'Hare was arrogant and standoffish, and Charlie was only too glad for O'Hare's visits to end.

Bud was now eighteen and beginning to find his way socially. Small communities in Wisconsin's north had few activities aside from working. Hunting and fishing were popular. But socially, dances and baseball games between communities were the primary recreation. And it was at a dance that Bud met a girl named Orma.

Bud and Orma were mere months apart in age. Both were small; Bud stood a mere 5-foot-4, Orma a petite 5-foot-2, and they shared similar interests. Orma was delighted to find a young man able to dance with such grace and ease. They were a perfect match on and off the dance floor, and their relationship grew.

Meanwhile, Charlie and Lola's relationship began to deteriorate. The two had fewer things to hold them together. With Velma and Bud now grown, and the work of erecting and maintaining the property completed, the couple found themselves arguing more. Lola, unable to drive, spent many days bored in her routine at the retreat while Charlie frequently disappeared for many hours or whole days at a time.

With Charlie away so much, out of loneliness and in desperation for companionship, Lola sometimes walked the six miles to Couderay village to visit some of her woman friends. These friends became more important to her and, eventually, would be vital to her life.

When Prohibition ended in 1933, Perry saw this as the time to break from his father's business. He and Velma moved to Couderay, where, with Charlie's help, they

built[94] and ran the Keystone bar.

While most of the building was erected using local stone, to add his own touch and a distinctive flare, Perry had slabs of granite shipped to create the keystones in the archways, hence the name, "Keystone" bar.

The bar was an immediate success, and Perry and Velma found themselves so busy in its operation that they hired a local woman, Mattie Patterson, to watch their three-year-old daughter, Shirley[95]. It was from this connection that a relationship between Charlie and Mattie began.

Mattie was 12 years younger than Charlie and married to Claude Patterson, a rough hulk of a man, who, besides being coarse and vulgar, was known throughout the community as abusive. So, it was natural for her to find an attraction in Charlie, who, although coarse himself, at least treated her with kindness.

With Perry's business thriving, he decided to expand. He heard that the Casino Dance Hall, found near Stone Lake, Wisconsin, 15 miles away, was for sale. Perry bought the building and, with the help of Charlie, Bud, and Charlie's friend Clarence Johnson, cut it into sections to move it.

Clarence began at ground level with his chainsaw. He cut up one wall, across the roof, and down the other side, dividing the building into three sections. Each section was loaded onto a heavy trailer and towed to where the building was reassembled at the outskirts of Couderay.

Renamed the Pixie Club[96], Perry's gamble paid off. People came from across Wisconsin's north to dance and be entertained by the many bands that played there.

It was at this time that Charlie learned of Goetz's murder.

Goetz had taken part in the kidnapping of a wealthy banker named Edward George Bremer. Earlier, in the summer of 1933, the Barker/Karpis gang kidnapped William Hamm, Jr., president of the Theodore Hamm Brewing Company, holding him for $100,000 ransom. By September, Goetz had become one of the gang members just when they pulled this second kidnapping[97].

The gang demanded $200,000 for Bremer's release Three weeks later, his family paid the ransom, and he was released. Although Bremer couldn't positively identify the kidnappers, he provided enough clues to lead police to suspect the Barker/Karpis gang.

It took nearly three months, but the police finally caught and questioned "Doc" Barker and his brother Fred. Released after questioning by police, yet worried that Goetz might talk, the brothers feared more evidence could turn up and that Goetz might squeal in exchange for a lighter sentence for himself. So, they contracted a hit.

Racing to find Goetz first, gunmen beat the feds to him in the town of Cicero. They shot him four times in the face with a shotgun at close range. He died instantly.

While this was happening, Charlie's work at the retreat continued, as did the decline of his and Lola's relationship.

Chapter 20
Fired!

Mattie Patterson was a pleasant, soft-spoken woman. With dark hair and a quick smile, she had endured years of neglect and abuse from her husband, Claude. This fact was well known in the community. Friends wondered how she was able to put up with him as long as she had, yet there were few options for women in this small community. Where could she go? Perhaps, Charlie was the answer.

Charlie often saw Mattie at the Keystone. And perhaps at other times. Her kind, easygoing personality added to her attractiveness. And Charlie's dislike for Mattie's husband was no secret. Many others in the community also shared this view.

As in most small communities, there were few secrets, and the relationship between Charlie and Mattie was whispered about freely. It was no secret to Lola either. But, like Mattie, she had few options. She too had to endure her husband's activities.

Bolton stated that the purpose of the massacre was to eliminate "Bugs" Moran, who had a gang which was the rival of the so-called Al Capone syndicate. He advised that the plans for the massacre were formulated at a resort owned by Fred Goetz on Cranberry Lake, six miles north of Couderay, Wisconsin during October or November, 1928. He stated that the following persons were present at this resort at the time the plans were made to kill "Bugs" Moran:

From FBI Memo

A second child, James, was born to Perry and Velma that fall. And the relationship between Bud and Orma became more serious. It wouldn't be long before Charlie and Lola had an empty nest and little to hold them together.

As 1934 came to an end, Byron Bolton and "Doc" Barker were captured in Chicago. Numerous charges faced them. Those against Bolton included the St. Valentine's Day Massacre, the murder of a police officer, a federal reserve robbery, and the Hamm and Bremer kidnappings.

Presented with a generous plea deal, Bolton was offered a few years in prison in exchange for information. He agreed, yielding that the purpose of the Saint Valentine's Day killing was to eliminate "Bugs" Moran from bootlegging in Chicago. Further, he claimed the plans were made "at a place on Cranberry Lake, 6 miles north of Couderey where one "George" operated a resort. (This was Goetz's alias of George Von Ash).

A few weeks later, on January 16, 1935, thanks to information provided by Bolton, the FBI raided a house in Oklawaha, Florida where "Ma" Barker and her son, Freddie, were hiding. Both were killed in a shootout with federal agents[98]. By May, after being named "Public Enemy Number 1", Alvin Karpis was captured.

As a further result of Bolton's testimony, his friend, "Doc" Barker, was sentenced to life in prison where he would die in 1939 while trying to escape from Alcatraz. So much for honor among thieves and refusing to talk.

In February of 1935, Bud and Orma married, living for a time with Charlie and Lola. It wasn't long though, before they decided on a move to southern Wisconsin where three of Orma's six brothers had found jobs. Bud hoped for the same. With US unemployment at nearly 25 percent, any opportunity for employment had to be considered.

Between The Great Depression and the devastating drought that caused the Dust Bowl of the Thirties, simple survival was a genuine worry for many. That being so, Charlie was fortunate to have his job at what was now O'Hare's retreat. Of course, Charlie also continued to supply venison for friends and to sell it whenever he could.

But then, early in 1936, thanks again to Bolton's statements, the FBI caught up to Charlie. They questioned him about his role in the acts of Goetz, O'Hare, and the others. But, as he had in the past, Charlie provided nothing of use, arguing that he was merely a caretaker. He, unlike Bolton, continued to protect his friends. After questioning, Charlie resumed his usual activities, though ever concerned about the eventual outcome.

From FBI Memo

Bolton stated that he knows these persons were at the resort because Goetz came to him and requested that he, Bolton, take a load of spaghetti and foodstuffs to the resort, and that these parties remained on the place at Cranberry Lake for two or three weeks, and this information can be verified by Frank Crandall and Eddy Anderson, guides who took the various individuals named hunting and fishing, and who lived in the vicinity of the resort. Charles Allison was a caretaker of the resort at that time and could also verify the presence of these various persons at that place.

In the ensuing months, Charlie heard nothing more from the FBI, or from any of those who had participated in the visits to the retreat – except for O'Hare. While coming only occasionally, his visits remained unannounced and brief. And upon each arrival, Charlie was questioned about whether there had been any visitors. Charlie, although not quite true, said that there hadn't been.

The truth was, Charlie sometimes invited friends from the area to fish or to simply enjoy the comparative luxury of the place. This was especially true following baseball games with neighboring communities in celebration of wins. But eventually, this practice caught up with him.

A baseball game against their rivals from Radisson, five miles east of Couderay, was an exciting one. The summer had been hot, and tempers were as well as the two teams battled for the season-ending championship. The teams were tied 5-5 in the bottom of the ninth with two men out. A Couderay runner stood on second base when a looping hit flew over the third-baseman's head and dropped into left field taking a high bounce. The fielder scooped up the ball and threw it as the runner rounded third. The ball and runner reached the plate together and when the dust settled, the catcher had dropped the ball. Couderay had won.

After a few minor scuffles and a lot of cheering, Charlie invited the entire team and their families to the retreat to celebrate. Others came as well. The players showered in the basement while children swam in the lake. Beer flowed and the party went on into the evening.

Then, as the last of the guests drove away, O'Hare drove in. Exiting his car, he stormed into the building where he saw towels strewn about. Beer bottles and trash lay scattered throughout the building and on the grounds. Furiously confronting Charlie, O'Hare said, "I told you, no visitors. I meant no visitors. You're fired! Get out, now!"

Chapter 21
Transition

Given only enough time to pack their belongings, Charlie and Lola left that night. With few other options, they went to Velma and Perry, who offered them a place to stay for the next few months.

In those months, Charlie negotiated to buy a tavern in the village – Dave's Place. Charlie renamed it Charlie's Bar. He would not be in direct competition with Perry's Keystone, because Perry's trade focused on evening business with vacationers, while Charlie's Bar served the local working-class. Thus, the tavern supplied Charlie and Lola not only an income but a place to live. This was fortunate because Velma was pregnant again.

Once Charlie's business was well established, he was too busy to have more than fleeting thoughts of the men he once worked with. Glad to be away from the need for vigilance, he enjoyed his new role as barkeeper. But he soon found himself busy with more than bartending. Vacationing fishermen sought bait for everything from crappies and bass to the large muskies that lurked in the Flambeau and Chippewa rivers. Here was another opportunity.

Charlie established a bait business along with his tavern. Through the summer months, he sold minnows trapped from the Couderay River. Lining his garage with large wooden barrels, he kept thousands of minnows sorted by type and size. Water pipes above the barrels fitted with nozzles sprayed water to freshen and aerate them. By the summer of 1939, this business, too, was flourishing.

By November, word reached Charlie that O'Hare was dead. A little more than a week before Capone's release from prison – on November 16, 1939 – O'Hare was shot and killed[99]. His murder occurred on a Wednesday as O'Hare left his office at Sportsman's Park racetrack in Cicero, Illinois. While driving his new Lincoln-Zephyr coupe, another car pulled next to him, and a shotgun blast from it hit him just below the ear. Another entered his neck. Reportedly, he was carrying a .32-caliber semi-automatic pistol, something he rarely did. But he never had a chance to reach for it. He was dead before his car stopped.

Capone was released from prison eight days later, having served seven and a half years. Many believed he ordered O'Hare killed for informing on him, but no arrests were ever made.

During the ensuing two years, tourism increased in northern Wisconsin. This enabled Charlie to add gas pumps and a billiard table to his tavern and bait business. And, as his business grew, his relationship with Mattie continued to grow, as well.

Mattie was still tending Velma and Perry's children, who, by then, numbered three. And Bud was working in a tobacco warehouse in southern Wisconsin. He and Orma now had two boys.

In that first year of their move to Janesville, Bud and Orma occupied the back room of a second-floor apartment shared with the family of one of her brothers. By the second year, they moved in with another brother whose home had more space.

The war in Europe was heating up, and it wouldn't be long before America would be drawn in. The demand for wheat and other products grew, and the opportunity for jobs grew as well. Because of this, Bud soon found a job at Fairbanks – Morse in Beloit, Wisconsin, assembling engines for ships and submarines. With this steady income, he was soon able to build his own home.

The coming war provided an opportunity for Charlie, as well. A highway through Canada to Alaska had been under consideration since the 1920s, and with war on the horizon, plans rapidly took shape. And though construction had not yet begun, other ventures were moving forward. Among them were several military bases in Alaska.

Gen. Simon Buckner Jr[100], as commander of the Army's Alaska Defense Command, was assigned to fortify and protect Alaska. His orders were to build Army and Army Air Corps bases at Anchorage.

However, he believed that bases in the Aleutian Islands were more vital to the defense of the U.S. west coast. Washington refused to agree. His requests to build the airfields he wanted were repeatedly turned down.

With a task so great and an army not yet large enough to complete the assignment, civilian construction crews were needed. As a result, hordes of construction workers began to ship into Alaskan ports. Soon, Charlie would join them.

Chapter 22

Alaska

Against orders, General Buckner covertly began Airfield construction in locations other than that authorized in September of 1941. He contracted with Morrison-Knudsen Construction Company, using diverted Civil Aeronautics Authority (CAA) funding under the Civilian Force Account. Although these actions were not approved until after the Pearl Harbor attack, supplies and equipment were shipped to the fictitious "Saxton and Company," a supposed cannery operation.

He hired construction teams from the lower 48 because of the scarcity of local labor, and because of his racial bias toward minorities, including Blacks and Yup'iks. He knew the war effort would require men and materiel in great numbers.

Buckner was gambling, for he knew he could be charged with embezzlement. Still, he began to stretch his protective bases farther west, along the Aleutian Islands. Although the attack on Pearl Harbor had yet to come, he was certain that war with Japan was inevitable.

One might see Buckner's actions as an example of unlawful acts committed for a good purpose, in some ways similar to Capone's "tainted" money used to feed the hungry through his Chicago soup kitchens.

As a no-nonsense soldier, Buckner – who would later command the Tenth army and die while directing the attack on Okinawa[101] – demanded a lot from his men. With a booming voice and a lack of tact, he inspired them by his own spartan lifestyle, bathing each morning in icy cold water in an outdoor tub, and making his headquarters in a tent rather than a downtown apartment. Such actions proved his willingness to suffer along with his men.

The war in Europe had caused many changes here at home. As war spread and worry consumed so many, Charlie's business began to flag until he was forced to seek more work or lose his business. When he learned of substantial pay offered to those willing to endure the harsh weather and spare conditions of construction work in Alaska, it didn't take him long to decide. Although he was then 54, Charlie was still strong and unafraid of rough conditions or rough men. He was going to Alaska.

This meant leaving Lola to take care of business once again while he was away for an unknown period. At least, with winter near, she would not have to deal with the minnow business or large numbers of customers.

Charlie arrived on the West Coast by train in time to board a ship leaving for Alaska. On it were other men seeking the same things – high pay and adventure. Their trip north was uneventful. Their arrival was less so as they passed through the Gulf of Alaska in high winds and rolling waves.

The ship entered Prince Edward Sound, docking at Port Whittier where Charlie saw vast shiploads of material addressed to Saxton & Company and marked "Cannery Equipment." Bulldozers and graders were included in this equipment, yet none of it was for a cannery. Port Whittier, Charlie learned, was a secret facility known as H-12, chosen for its access to rail service and because it remained ice-free all year.

They disembarked in harsh weather, which soon became much worse. Snowfall at Whittier averaged 260 inches per year, and rainfall was 174

inches.

As soon as the men were off the ship and settled into Quonset or Pacific huts, they were put to work. Their first task was to register their skills and receive assignments.

Although civilians, their supervisors were officials of the CAA[102]. The men were organized military style and placed in units made up of carpenters, electricians, plumbers, and others, thus allowing units to handle each of the tasks necessary for its assigned project. The building of runways was left to the Seabees. Charlie, assigned as a carpenter, helped erect barracks and other buildings. Then, as the housing neared completion, his experience building roads in the Chicago area was discovered and he was reassigned to operate heavy equipment. Simple things, such as roads, were vital to moving

material for all the projects.

One of those early projects was supposed to be constructing McGrath Army Airbase. But the ground had frozen solid by the time the equipment arrived, so Buckner diverted material for that project to Cold Bay to construct Fort Randall Army Airfield[103], and to Umnak to build Cape Field. Because of Buckner's foresight, these bases were completed in time to defend against the Japanese air attack on Dutch Harbor.

Charlie, fortunately, would be spared involvement in any of the attacks by Japanese forces. He did, however, suffer from the cold. Rain, snow, and gale-force winds made working conditions nearly unbearable. Proper clothing was scarce, and very costly.

He was paid very well though, as he had expected, and he sent a small portion of his pay to Couderay to help Lola get by. But he also sent a part to Mattie. He and Mattie had kept in touch, writing back and forth. Lola knew nothing of this, but

the postmaster in the village did. And so, subtle rumors began to spread.

Chapter 23
Rumors

In Couderay, Lola continued to manage the tavern. Business had improved through the summer as fishermen and other vacationers returned, but Lola was unable to trap minnows as Charlie had, so she engaged the help of some teenage boys, sharing the proceeds with them.

As summer came and left, Charlie's letters arrived less often. His unknown period away had stretched into months.

Winter 1941 neared, and customers were scarce again as men returned to the woods to cut timber. The busiest time at the tavern was weekends when the regulars dropped in to drink, play cards, and catch up on events. This provided hardly enough income to support the business, although it also meant fewer expenses in stocking the bar. Lola's financial needs were mainly for food and fuel oil.

Letters between Charlie and Lola had little to say, aside from Lola's need for money. When Charlie did write, he sometimes enclosed small checks, but always stressed the difficult working conditions. More often, he sent money to Bud for safekeeping. It was to Mattie he wrote most often.

The postmaster in Couderay was aware that Charlie was sending letters to both Lola and Mattie. That information should have remained unknown to others, yet somehow, word was whispered about. Lola suspected as much but had no interest in a confrontation. She was hopeful that, in time, things would get better.

It was then that rumors of impending war came true. The Japanese struck Pearl Harbor on December 7. The next day, Germany declared war on the United States.

Charlie was building wharfs and jetties at that time, as the importance of expanding Alaskan ports had reached a new level. Crews were scheduled to work around the clock to prepare against an invasion. And because of the attack, it would be many more months before Charlie could consider returning home.

Six months after the raid on Pearl Harbor, the Japanese attacked and bombed the Alaskan port city of Dutch Harbor. This was followed by the invasion and occupation of the islands[104] of Attu and Kiska. Ten men from a U. S. Navy weather station were on Kiska. Two were killed, seven captured. One eluded capture for nearly two months before cold and hunger forced him, reduced to just 80 pounds, to surrender[105].

It would be nearly a year before U. S. forces were able to retake Attu[106] in Operation Land Crab,[107] one of the deadliest battles of World War II. The fighting lasted 18 days, and in the end, all but 29 Japanese were killed. Military activity had reached a new level as men and equipment poured into the area. But Charlie was never in danger. His life remained a simple, daily grind of cold, wetness, and work.

Still, there was constant fear that the Japanese would invade and establish a beachhead somewhere along the Alaska coast. And while Alaska Natives were generally considered unreliable, it became apparent that their skills, knowledge of the terrain, and conditioning to the weather made them ideal for the task of coast watchers. Men and women alike were veteran hunters and trackers who knew how to shoot, and so the Alaska Territorial Guard was formed around them[108].

Native villagers were forcibly removed from the islands by American troops and placed into camps on Admiralty Island after some Aleuts from Attu were taken prisoner by the Japanese. There, although they received poor treatment by the U. S. government, they quickly volunteered to serve in the Territorial Guard lest they be seen as unpatriotic.

Charlie met some subsistence hunters from the island of Unalaska[109]. He bartered with one of them for a piece of scrimshaw the man had carved on a walrus tusk. It was in the form of a cribbage board, and it served Charlie well during the next several months.

The long winter nights changed to long summer days before Charlie's job finally ended in August of 1943 and he returned home to Couderay. Lola was glad he was back, although their relationship hadn't improved. Charlie acted bitter toward her. However, the tavern was doing a moderate trade, and once Charlie got his bait business running again, traffic improved.

As Charlie caught up on events at home, he learned that Frank Nitti had committed suicide five months earlier. Interestingly, Nitti was buried at Mount Carmel Cemetery in Hillside, Illinois, close to the grave of Al Capone, with the graves of Dean O'Banion and Hymie Weiss nearby.

Charlie had done well in Alaska, bringing substantial earnings back with him. For Lola, he brought nothing. But when Bud came from Janesville for a visit, Charlie presented him with the scrimshaw he had bartered for.

Because the war in Europe continued and farms there became battlefields, a system of rationing had been implemented in the United States, beginning with tires[110]. By the time Charlie returned from Alaska, numerous other goods had been added to the list, including meat. This gave Charlie an opportunity to, once again, sell venison on the black market. Between the tavern and his other interests, Charlie kept busy, allowing him and Lola to manage a distant relationship for some time.

Mattie's relationship to her husband, Claude, continued to decline, as well. They had four children together, though only one remained at home.

By the fall of 1944, Charlie's tavern was thriving. He added a billiard table to encourage customers to linger and to draw in younger people. It worked. Because few activities were available in the area, this added a new dimension. Pool proved to be especially popular with hunters and gamblers

Deer hunting had been closed or greatly restricted through the 1930s[111], but with timber wolves nearing extinction and other predators rare, deer were enjoying a resurgence. And deer hunting brought Bud back for another visit in November.

He discovered Charlie and Lola living together under a strained relationship. This was not altogether a surprise, but it was disappointing. One year later, in November of 1945, the friction between them was more apparent to Bud, yet he was not prepared for what would soon follow.

Chapter 24
Break Up

In August of 1945, Bud and Orma had had a fourth child, their third boy. Their home was becoming too small for their growing family. With the war over, Bud's job in the war industry had ended. But he had saved enough money during the war to be without a job until the end of the year, then he was to start a new job at a tobacco warehouse.

With his time and savings, Bud added a second story to their small home, including three bedrooms and a bath. While completing the roof, a local businessman stopped by. He had watched Bud's progress regularly, and he offered Bud a job with his roofing company. Bud answered that he had plenty of work to do for now but would keep his offer in mind. They parted with Bud having a standing offer of a job.

In November, Bud drove north to hunt deer and visit with his parents. By then, things were coming to a head between the two, as it was with Mattie and Claude.

As usual, Bud was greeted warmly, but the chill between Charlie and Lola was obvious. Bitter words were exchanged freely, especially by Charlie. This made Bud very uncomfortable, so immediately after harvesting the venison his family needed, he ended his visit and returned home.

As the new year began, Charlie and Lola's marriage ended. It was January 1946. Charlie closed the tavern for the night and entered that part of the tavern that was their home. He said to Lola, "Get out, now! I've had enough."

"Charlie!"

"I mean it."

"What do mean, Charlie?"

"You know what I mean. We're through. I've put up with you as long as I'm going to. Now, get your stuff and get out!"

"But Charlie, it's the middle of winter. Where am I to go? It's freezing out."

"Get out!"

"I haven't any money, Charlie."

"That's too bad. You damn sure aren't getting any from me."

"But where'll I go?"

"You can go to hell, for all I care," he said in a rage. "You've got fifteen minutes to get your things and get out or I'll kill you!"

Lola, frightened for her life, quickly gathered a few items of clothing in a suitcase, took up her coat and scarf, and went out into the cold December night. Uncertain what to do or where to go, she toted her belongings to the home of her closest friend, Julia.

Knocking on the door, Lola stood in the cold for several minutes before a light finally came on. Invited in, Lola related her tale to Julia, who offered Lola a bed for the night.

In the morning, at breakfast, Julia offered to purchase a railroad ticket for Lola to travel to Janesville. Grateful for the offer, Lola felt she had no choice but to accept. And so, late on a January afternoon, Lola was on a train headed to Janesville, in southern Wisconsin where she hoped Bud and Orma would provide shelter, at least for a time.

And Charlie? Rid of his wife of thirty-seven years, he was free to pursue his other interest, Mattie.

Lola arrived in Janesville near midnight, January 6. The small city appeared to be asleep. Bud's home at the north edge of the city was two miles from the train depot, and there was no way for Lola to get there but to walk. Bud and Orma had no telephone. Stepping from the train, Lola took up her suitcase and set out.

The night was clear and cold, but fortunately, no recent snow. She arrived outside Bud and Orma's home shortly after one a.m. She was very cold. Her hands were nearly frozen. Lola rapped on the door.

Bud and Orma lay asleep in their downstairs bedroom. Orma, hearing the rap, awoke, wondering who could be there at that hour. She got up to investigate while Bud continued to sleep. Without turning on a light, she went to the door where, through a window, she saw a figure silhouetted against the snowy background. Turning on the porch light, she was surprised to see Lola standing there.

"Lola," she said, as she opened the door. "What in the world are you doing here? What happened? Come in here. You must be frozen."

"Oh, Orma," Lola said. "It's awful. Charlie kicked me out."

"What?"

"It's true, Orma. He threatened to kill me if I didn't go."

The two sat together at the kitchen table while Lola related her tale. Talking through the night, Lola told Orma everything. She added, though, that she didn't want Bud to know of his father's threat to her.

"I don't want Buddy to turn against his father. It's enough to know that we separated."

When Bud arose, expecting to begin the day at his new job, he was surprised to see his mother sitting at the table with Orma. She told him briefly that she and Charlie decided to separate, and that she needed a place to stay. Bud, said, of course Lola could stay with them, suggesting the two older boys could share a bedroom. That decided, Orma made arrangements for his mother as Bud left for his new job at the tobacco warehouse.

As the week progressed, Bud learned more of the story, but only that Charlie and Lola had agreed to separate. Lola never mentioned the worst parts, for she truly didn't want Bud to be angry with his father.

Mattie felt her children were old enough to cope without her now, the youngest being a teen, and she was tired of taking abuse from her husband, Claude. Perhaps she and Charlie had planned this, or it may have been coincidence, but in any case, she soon moved in with Charlie at the tavern and this arrangement continued from that day.

Claude was not troubled by Mattie's leaving. Their marriage had never been a good one, and he, too, was now free to pursue life unencumbered.

Chapter 25

A New Start

Within that year, 1946, Lola was well settled with Bud's family, glad to help with the children. It was the first time in her life that she had known relative ease. She was happy.

While Lola was starting her new life in Janesville, Charlie and Mattie were living together in Couderay. At 45, Mattie was 12 years younger than Charlie. Their age difference meant nothing to them. They enjoyed each other's company, and that was enough. Charlie continued to run his tavern while Mattie joined him behind the bar.

Perry had sold the Keystone two years earlier, closed the Pixie Club, and moved with Velma to California to start a new business. While the Keystone continued operation under a new owner, the Pixie Club was boarded up and abandoned for several years.

In November, the fall after Lola's moving in with Bud and Orma, Bud arrived in Couderay for the deer hunting season. He didn't stay with Charlie and Mattie though. Instead, he spent nights at a resort near Birchwood run by Orma's brother, Lester. Bud's visits with Charlie and Mattie were warm and cordial, and little was said of his parents' separation. Mattie was well known to Bud, who gave tacit approval to their relationship.

As they caught up on the latest news and shared stories of the past, Bud enjoyed a few beers. But Charlie rarely drank beer. Rather, a bottle of whiskey was always at hand, as was his ever-present cigar. It was clear that Charlie enjoyed the tavern business. His gruff demeanor seemed a perfect fit for the rough crowd that often frequented his bar. He was adept at telling stories, prefaced by taking up his ever-present gray fedora, slapping it on his head, and starting off in his loud, gravelly voice. All other voices were stilled when he spoke, for it was clear that he meant to be heard.

These visits always ended more quietly, with talk of family and the future.

In parting, Charlie was never one for kind words, especially words of affection. The closest he came might be exemplified by an occasion years later, when a grandson and his wife were leaving, and Mattie said to them in her gentle voice, "Please, come back soon. We so look forward to your visits. And you know Charlie and I both love you, even though Charlie would never say so."

To which Charlie harrumphed, saying, "Well, all I have to say is, Mattie might do a lot of things, but one thing she never does is lie."

So, while Charlie was normally gruff and ready to argue with anyone else, Mattie had a quieting influence on him.

Orma's youngest brother, Delbert, mustered out of the Army early in 1947, having served with the Occupation forces in Japan. But, as a young man, Delbert had no home to return to. So, Bud and Orma welcomed him into theirs until he could get settled. This made for a cramped household, but Lola had received an offer to cook at Elmer's Café in downtown Janesville. Accepting the offer, she moved into an apartment near the café, making room for Delbert.

Lola enjoyed her work at the restaurant. There she met people from all walks – businessmen, attorneys, salespeople, railway laborers. She developed a wide circle of friends, and her life went on uneventfully until one day in 1952 when a man entered wearing a familiar brown business suit and a fedora.

Startled at first, Lola said, "Nick! Is that you?"

"Hello, Lola."

"Oh my god, Nick! You've hardly changed. What are you doing here?"

"I heard you were here; that you and Charlie had separated."

"How could you? How would you know where to find me?" she asked.

"You forget. That's my job, finding people. It's good to see you, Lola. How have you been?"

The two caught up briefly before Nick left, only to return later when Lola was through work. Over the ensuing days, they became reacquainted and made plans before Nick had to leave to carry on with his business. He would return.

Chapter 26
California

It was at this time that Bud began the laborious task of building a garage of concrete block with the help of Orma and their oldest son, 16-year-old Ken. Bud's design for the garage included an apartment above for Lola, and the next spring, she moved in to her new home.

For Charlie, the years after Lola's departure were among the most peaceful he had known. His life had become more routine and sedate. But he was older now, and at 66, he was ready to retire. Selling the tavern, he and Mattie moved to California to be close to Perry and Velma, and where Charlie was offered a job managing an apartment building.

Because the position came with a free apartment, Charlie accepted the job. But it was only a matter of months before he found himself bombarded with requests and complaints from tenants. Not one to take orders from others, he soon quit this job and turned to trucking, hauling mobile homes cross-country.

In the fall of 1952, Nick returned to Janesville, and he and Lola set out to visit many parts of the United States together. Their first destination was Arizona, away from Wisconsin's wintery weather. Carlsbad Caverns in New Mexico was next on their journey. Then, on their drive back to Wisconsin, they visited Mitchell, South Dakota, where Lola was awed by the Corn Palace. She returned home excited about her adventure and rich with tales to tell. With Nick, she had enjoyed the best year of her life before he, once again, left on business.

It was months later when Nick reappeared, as mysteriously as ever. He and Lola left together again this time to Kentucky for a visit to Mammoth Cave. For Lola, it was as though she had a new start on life. Although she was then 65, she felt much younger.

Upon their return, Nick left on another of his secretive business trips. As usual, though, he kept in touch with Lola through frequent letters. But then, his letters suddenly stopped. Lola was at a loss. He had simply disappeared.

More than a year passed before a letter arrived from one of Nick's daughters. In it, Lola learned that Nick was dead. He was killed in Chicago. Shot down. Lola was devastated. Her life was turned upside down. At least, she had some closure. Nick hadn't simply left her. But he had left his mark.

It took Lola months to recover from this disturbing event, but eventually found she had to busy herself with something. So, in 1956, she bought a large wooden-frame loom on which to make rag rugs. Rags were plentiful and easy to come by, and soon she was cutting and sewing together one-inch-wide strips, organized by color. From these bits of cloth, she found a ready market for her rugs, and spent many hours at her loom, where she could look out her front window and listen to baseball on the radio. This became her life.

Charlie's age was catching up to him. Tired of the long drives, tired of working, and tired of being away from Mattie so much, he decided on another change. So, after talking with Perry and Velma, he decided to return to Wisconsin and the woods of Couderay, where Perry still owned the abandoned Pixie Club. With some work, it could be turned into a decent home, Charlie thought, so, a deal was quickly struck. Perry transferred ownership to Charlie, and he and Mattie prepared for their move back to Couderay.

Chapter 27

Return to Couderay

Once they arrived in Couderay, Charlie had the well and septic system restored. With the addition of some appliances and a few pieces of furniture, the Pixie Club was transformed into a modest home for Mattie and him. The rest of the village had changed little.

Charlie was happy to be back in Wisconsin. Mattie was glad, too, for she would again be near her two youngest boys and her long-time friends. The pace of life was much more relaxed in Couderay, too; something they missed while in California.

Charlie discovered something else upon their return. He found that the life he had lived was catching up with him. He tired more easily. His once thick red hair had become a fringe of gray. His heavy, horn-rimmed glasses seemed heavier, and he spent much of his time idle as his strength was ebbing. Charlie still enjoyed his cigars and whiskey, though, and his voice retained its gruff tone.

Bud renewed his summer visits, and always for deer season, staying at a cottage he had built near Birchwood. The two enjoyed reliving events together.

"After you was born down in Springfield," Charlie said, "with you and all of us nearly dying, those were hard times. And the coal mines, they were the worst. Then Chicago. You remember any of that?"

"I don't remember the names of any of the kids I went to school with. They were a tough bunch. And I remember that fellow with no feet."

"Pearl Robinson," Charlie interjected. "Wasn't he a character? Legs cut off at the knees. Damn hard worker though, I liked him."

"And the fire," Bud said, "the one at the hotel. I was just seven then, I think, but I remember that. I remember people rushing around, and the smell, the smoke."

"Bud? Care for another beer?" Mattie asked.

"Yeah, I'll have one."

"And you, Charlie, I know you still have your whiskey," Mattie smiled.

"Then there was the fire at the old beanery," Charlie added. "I wonder what happened to those White brothers, the bastards! Never so glad to leave a city in my life. Never went back either."

"The tavern was good to you, Charlie," Mattie said.

"I guess. Never liked working for nobody else," he said, adding, "had some fun there though. A few good people. But then there was those like old Ernie Bielinski. Always sat at the end of the bar. He could nurse a beer for hours."

"Oh," Mattie said, "I remember him. Tightfisted man?"

"Tightfisted, hell. A skinflint! Last time he was in, a few others there, too, each'd buy a round of drinks and Ernie'd say, 'I'll pass.' Each time he'd say that, round after round. Then comes time for him to leave, he says to me, 'I'll take my money now.' I says, 'What money?' He says, 'For each of the beers I passed on. I count seven of them, so I'll take my money for them now.'" Charlie said, "I kicked that son-of-a-bitch out and told him to never come back, and he didn't."

They laughed and shared more tales of the past, the good and the bad. "By Christ, those were the times, weren't they, Bud?"

Mattie chimed in, saying, "You've had a hard road, Charlie."

"You're damn right it's been hard."

"Reminds me, I better hit the road," Bud said, finishing his beer. "Deer hunting in the morning."

Charlie longed to be back in the woods hunting too. Until recently, he would go into the woods briefly, usually skipping opening day. He loved the freedom he felt in the woods, yet now waited until mid-season before venturing out for an afternoon or two, when there was less hunting pressure. And even then, he targeted young deer for their tenderness, and because they were easier to drag from the woods.

The next few years were quiet ones for Charlie and Mattie. Life became a matter of simple routine, fishing, short walks, gardening and, of course, the fall hunt.

O'Hare's retreat had been shuttered for several years; ownership taken over by the Chippewa Valley Bank. But in 1959, an enterprising man named Guy Houston bought the 407-acre property. His goal was to turn it into a tourist attraction called "The Hideout," where, for a small fee, patrons were taken on a guided tour of the grounds seeing a glimpse of what was purported to be "Capone's Hideout."

Chapter 28
Realization

Charlie and Lola had never formally divorced. Now, in his 70s, Charlie began thinking of his inevitable death and the need to leave his worldly goods to others. He had Bud and Velma to consider, and Mattie had her children, too. Although separated for years, Charlie felt he and Lola should eliminate potential probate issues, so he wrote to her.

Lola was surprised when she received Charlie's letter after so many years apart, yet she readily saw the wisdom of it. After all, she had things to pass along, too, although everything would go to Bud for having taken her in. Still, the legal documents would reassure her.

Lola agreed with Charlie's request, and the divorce was quickly accomplished. Not long after, in 1965, Charlie, 78, and Mattie, 66, married.

In the years that followed, Charlie faced other concerns. His health began to deteriorate. He often felt unwell, weak, even depressed. Some days he didn't bother to dress; he simply sat in his chair while wrapped in a robe. And as he became more dependent, he became more despondent.

He often complained that his best days were behind him. And they were, for, one day, Mattie noticed something and asked Charlie about it.

"Charlie. I need to ask you something. Are you feeling all right?"

"Whatta you mean, Mattie? I feel good enough."

"Blood, Charlie. I been finding blood in your shorts when I do your laundry."

"Hemorrhoids, that's all. I got piles."

"Charlie, I've been doing your clothes a long time now. I've seen blood in your shorts before, but not like this. I think you need to see a doctor."

"Doctor, hell! I ain't going to no damn doctor. They'd just find something and give me some pills."

But she eventually convinced him, and he was right, they found something. Cancer. He needed surgery. A colostomy. The procedure was extensive and left Charlie with a stoma for the collection of waste.

The surgery further weakened Charlie. Walking became an effort. His recovery took months. He had been strong and capable for much of his life, but now was severely limited, in pain, and angry.

"Mattie," he said. "I can't do anything. I'm shitting into a bag. I stink. This is no way for a man to live. I'm through. I'm ready to give up."

"You can't give up, Charlie. We can still do things."

But it was hard for both. Yet, Charlie didn't give up. He couldn't give up. Not yet anyway. His heart was in the north, in the woods and the lakes. And another deer season had arrived. He wanted to return to the woods once more. Mattie tried to talk him out of it, but it was useless. He would do what he wanted. Nobody could change his mind about this, not even Mattie.

So, mid-week of the 1975 deer season, she helped him dress in his heavy woolen clothing, and they drove to a secluded spot where he could walk from the car to a slight knoll along the edge of the woods. It was a struggle, even with Mattie carrying his rifle for him. He found a tall oak overlooking a marshy thicket, and there he sat, his back against the tree.

Mattie returned to the car to wait. She didn't have to wait long. In little more than an hour, she heard Charlie call to her. He was through.

Helping him back to the car, he said, "That's it, Mattie. I can't do it no more. Take me home." His spirit was finally broken.

Later that week, Bud, back home in Janesville, received a phone call from Mattie. "Bud, you need to come up here. We have to do something. I can't manage Charlie any longer."

Chapter 29

All But Forgotten

When Bud arrived, he found his father sitting in a dimly lit room, appearing shrunken, hardly the man he used to be. Charlie's voice was weak at first, but grew in intensity as he said, "I'm tied to this damn thing with shit coming out of my belly. The damn thing leaks. I stink. I can't live this way anymore, Bud."

"What do you want to do, Dad?"

"Die! What else is there?"

"Charlie!" Mattie exclaimed. "Don't say that. You still have things to live for. I need you. Don't talk about dying."

"What else can I do? I can barely walk. It's hard to eat. Any friends I ever had are all dead. I'm next."

The three talked for some time before Charlie finally settled down and Bud was able to share about the rest of the family. But before Bud went back to his summer cottage near Birchwood, Charlie whispered to him, "I still want to die."

He didn't die, of course. Not yet. But Bud knew death wasn't far off. Mattie was developing health issues of her own and could no longer give Charlie the care he needed. So, with what seemed like no other recourse, Bud arranged for Charlie to enter a complete care facility in Rice Lake.

Once there, Charlie became angry, bitter, belligerent. Enraged, he was soon throwing things, aggressively striking out at the nurses, swearing at them, and pulling his IVs out. He had to be restrained. This was the final blow for Charlie, a man who had always been wildly independent. He refused to be tamed, yet now, fighting to the last, his spirit suddenly died, and soon after, on September 9, 1977, so did his body. Charlie Allison was 90. His struggles were over.

Ended was a life of hardship. Led by his own sense of survival, Charlie had always done whatever he felt was necessary. He left his foster parents, walking away from their cruelty. He fought those who tried to dominate him, whether schoolteachers, bullies, or bosses. He worked hard and developed the skills he needed to compete and complete whatever challenges he faced. And he developed loyal friendships when friendships were necessary.

Chapter 30

Summation

To be sure, Charlie was no saint. He could be mean, even cruel at times. But something about him drew me to him, encouraging me to write about his life. Perhaps it was his strength. It may have been the gentleness I saw beneath his gruff exterior. Maybe it was nothing more than the fact that he was my grandfather. I don't know. What I do know is that he survived difficult times, times I doubt I could have lived through.

He, like so many others, struggled to make a living, doing what he felt was necessary, law or no law. Survival was his rule. Not only did Charlie survive, but he rubbed elbows with men of historical note, men read about, businessmen like any others except, as my grandmother said, "Their business was just against the law."

The exploits of those others have been remembered and written about many times, while Charlie's might be all but forgotten, though they shouldn't be. He was a part of their history, too. And so, this book.

It is my hope that those who read about Charlie Allison will think of others who came before, knowing that it is from their strength and willingness to do what was necessary that we are here.

---

[1] Originally Owain, meaning "well born" in old Celtic.

[2] http://www.illinoislaborhistory.org/labor-history-articles/early-days-of-coal-mining-in-northern-illinois

[3] https://sangamoncountyhistory.org/wp/?p=10565#:~:text=Bolton%20told%20the%20FBI%20in,14%2C%201929.

[4] https://www.tngenweb.org/campbell/hist-bogan/mules.html

[5] https://sangamoncountyhistory.org/wp/?p=412

[6] https://en.wikipedia.org/wiki/Illinois_Terminal_Railroad

[7] http://www.illinoislaborhistory.org/labor-history-articles/early-days-of-coal-mining-in-northern-illinois

[8] https://en.wikipedia.org/wiki/Battle_of_Virden

[9] https://www.lib.niu.edu/1995/ii950928.html

[10] https://hinton-gen.com/coal/macoupin_mines.html

[11] https://arippa.org/what-is-coal-refuse/

[12] https://arippa.org/what-is-coal-refuse/

[13] https://rouxbe.com/tips-techniques/331-spring-wheat-vs-winter-wheat

[14] https://en.wikipedia.org/wiki/Reaper-binder#:~:text=The%20binder%20was%20invented%20in,stems%20into%20bundles

[15] https://www.army.mil/article/185229/world_war_i_building_the_american_military

[16] https://encyclopedia.1914-1918-online.net/article/american_expeditionary_forces

[17] https://spartacus-educational.com/FWWusa.htm

[18] https://www.lib.ncsu.edu/news/special-collections/world-war-i-and-agriculture

[19] https://www.archives.gov/exhibits/influenza-epidemic/

[20] https://www.influenzaarchive.org/

[21] https://www.cdc.gov/flu/pandemic-resources/1918-pandemic-h1n1.html

[22] https://www.ncbi.nlm.nih.gov/pmc/articles/PMC2600384/

[23] http://mafiasome.blogspot.com/2015/05/shotgun-george-ziegler.html

[24] http://homebrewedmojo.blogspot.com/2017/03/the-hidden-life-of-fred-goetz.html

[25] http://www.myalcaponemuseum.com/id107.htm

[26] https://www.history.com/news/10-things-you-should-know-about-prohibition

[27] https://www.britannica.com/biography/Johnny-Torrio

[28] https://archive.org/stream/BremerKidnapping/Bremer%20Kidnapping%20193_djvu.txt

[29]   https://vault.fbi.gov/barker-karpis-gang/bremer-investigation-summary/Barker-Karpis%20Gang%20Summary%20Part%201%20of%201

[30] https://en.wikipedia.org/wiki/Chicago_Outfit

[31] https://honors11.tripod.com/id1.html

[32] https://en.wikipedia.org/wiki/Dean_O%27Banion

[33] https://en.wikipedia.org/wiki/Dean_O%27Banion

[34]   https://www.npr.org/2012/02/14/146862081/the-history-of-the-fbis-secret-enemies-list

[35]   https://www.fbi.gov/history/brief-history/the-fbi-and-the-american-gangster#:~:text=In%20one%20big%20city%20alone,off%20politicians%20and%20po

[36] https://en.wikipedia.org/wiki/Genna_crime_family

[37] https://themobmuseum.org/notable_names/dean-obanion/

[38] https://en.wikipedia.org/wiki/Genna_crime_family

[39] https://en.wikipedia.org/wiki/Dean_O%27Banion

[40]   http://chicagocrimescenes.blogspot.com/2008/09/obanions-flower-shop.html

[41] https://en.wikipedia.org/wiki/Dean_O%27Banion

[42] https://themobmuseum.org/notable_names/dean-obanion/

[43] https://en.wikipedia.org/wiki/North_Side_Gang

[44] https://www.britannica.com/biography/Johnny-Torrio

[45] https://americanmafiahistory.com/giovanni-papa-johnny-torrio/

[46] https://en.wikipedia.org/wiki/Johnny_Torrio

[47]   https://prohibition.themobmuseum.org/the-history/the-prohibition-underworld/bootleggers-and-bathtub-gin/

[48]   https://prohibition.themobmuseum.org/the-history/the-prohibition-underworld/bootleggers-and-bathtub-gin/

[49] https://www.wpr.org/farming-logging-shaped-wisconsins-identity

[50] https://en-academic.com/dic.nsf/enwiki/732744

[51] https://www.findagrave.com/memorial/73018274/theodore-anton

[52]   https://www.google.com/books/edition/The_Outfit/GnCn1u-zHbQC?hl=en&gbpv=1&dq=1927+restaurant+manager+at+the+hawthor

[53] https://en.wikipedia.org/wiki/Frankie_Yale

[54] https://www.nationalcrimesyndicate.com/day-1930-joe-aiello-killed-aged-39/

[55] https://medium.com/@andrew_ward/capones-foes-joey-aiello-1615c061df2f

[56] https://en.wikipedia.org/wiki/1927_in_organized_crime

[57] https://amp.freejournal.info/10419933/1/sheldon-gang.html

[58] http://chicagocrimescenes.blogspot.com/2009/05/antonio-lombardo-killed-in-loop.html

[59] https://en.wikipedia.org/wiki/Joe_Aiello

[60] https://en.wikipedia.org/wiki/Antonio_Lombardo

[61] https://ampoleagle.com/the-man-that-al-capone-feared-p10397-208.htm

[62] https://en.wikipedia.org/wiki/1927_in_organized_crime

[63] https://en.wikipedia.org/wiki/Timeline_of_organized_crime_in_Chicago

[64] https://en.wikipedia.org/wiki/Frankie_Yale

[65] https://en.wikipedia.org/wiki/Rice_Lake,_Dallas_and_Menomonie_Railway

[66] https://sangamoncountyhistory.org/wp/?p=10565

[67] https://en.wikipedia.org/wiki/Saint_Valentine%27s_Day_Massacre#Other_suspects

[68] http://www.myalcaponemuseum.com/id91.htm

[69] https://stvalentinemassacre.org/fred-killer-burke/#full

[70] http://www.myalcaponemuseum.com/id41.htm

[71] https://crime-and-corruption.fandom.com/wiki/Frank_%22The_Enforcer%22_Nitti

[72] https://en.wikipedia.org/wiki/Gus_Winkler

[73] https://www.worthpoint.com/worthopedia/press-photo-ralph-bottles-capone-1807043680

[74] https://theclio.com/entry/769011

[75] https://sangamoncountyhistory.org/wp/?p=10565 - Bolton told the FBI, planning for the massacre began in the fall of 1928 at a resort Goetz ran in Wisconsin.

[76] https://en.wikipedia.org/wiki/Bugs_Moran#Battling_Al_Capone

[77]   http://chicagocrimescenes.blogspot.com/2008/11/capones-cicero-headquarters.html

[78] https://themobmuseum.org/blog/machine-gun-jack-mcgurn-leads-lists-of-top-5-most-notorious-mob-hitmen/

[79] https://sangamoncountyhistory.org/wp/?p=10565

[80]   http://www.anvari.org/fortune/Miscellaneous_Collections/399720_nobody-shot-me-frank-gusenberg-his-last-words-when-asked-by-police-who-had-shot-him-14-times-with-a-machine-gun-in-the-saint-valentines-day-massacre.html

[81]   https://www.history.com/this-day-in-history/the-st-valentines-day-massacre

[82] https://famous-trials.com/alcapone/1475-chronology

[83] https://www.history.com/news/al-capone-great-depression-soup-kitchen

[84] http://www.myalcaponemuseum.com/id230.htm

[85] https://glitternight.com/2018/03/29/non-dillinger-shotgun-ziegler/

[86] https://www.americanmafia.com/Feature_Articles_218.html

[87] https://www.navytimes.com/news/your-navy/2018/12/26/the-incredible-life-and-terrible-death-of-the-navys-first-world-war-ii-ace/

[88] https://www.geni.com/people/Ursula-Nitti/6000000011908201493

[89] https://en.wikipedia.org/wiki/Edward_J._O%27Hare

[90] https://preacherpollard.com/2017/09/27/redemption-and-pearl-harbor/

[91] http://law2.umkc.edu/faculty/projects/ftrials/capone/caponeaccount.html

[92] https://www.fbi.gov/history/famous-cases/al-capone

[93] http://www.myalcaponemuseum.com/id246.htm

[94] 1933

[95] Born November 1930

[96] http://www.couderaywisconsin.com/history/businesses.htm

[97] https://www.fbi.gov/history/famous-cases/barker-karpis-gang

[98]   https://www.newspapers.com/clip/26405038/ma-and-fred-barker-killed-january-16/

[99] https://en.wikipedia.org/wiki/Edward_J._O%27Hare

[100] https://en.wikipedia.org/wiki/Simon_Bolivar_Buckner_Jr.

[101] https://en.wikipedia.org/wiki/Simon_Bolivar_Buckner_Jr.

[102] CAA - Civilian Aeronautics Authority

[103] http://www.airfields-freeman.com/AK/Airfields_AK.htm#ftrandall

[104] https://www.nps.gov/articles/world-war-ii-in-alaska.htm

[105] https://en.wikipedia.org/wiki/
Japanese_occupation_of_Kiska#:~:text=The%20Japanese%20occupation%20of%20Kiska,fla

[106] https://en.wikipedia.org/wiki/Battle_of_Attu

[107] https://www.nps.gov/articles/000/battle-of-attu-60-years.htm

[108] https://auntphilstrunk.com/eskimo-scouts-guard-alaska/

[109] https://www.nps.gov/articles/aleu-mobley-intro.htm

[110] https://www.nationalww2museum.org/war/articles/rationing

[111] https://dnr.wi.gov/topic/hunt/documents/deer4page.pdf

Don't miss out!

Visit the website below and you can sign up to receive emails whenever Don Allison publishes a new book. There's no charge and no obligation.

https://books2read.com/r/B-A-OETV-SKYCC

BOOKS 2 READ

Connecting independent readers to independent writers.

Also by Don Allison

Charlie

About the Author

Don Allison is a retired industrial process coordinator who left the work-world to begin life anew. That new life included writing, publishing, and television production.

He is the author of 2 other books, *The Black Bridge Road*, and *Walkers Hollow*. The first is a creative non-fiction book about a boy's adventures in the freedom-filled mid-America of the 1950s. The second is a fictional account of people and life in a small Wisconsin village, also in the 1950's, where nearly anything can happen.

Don currently lives in Janesville, Wisconsin with Lyn, his wife of 57 years.